HOPES AND DREAMS

An IEP Guide for Parents of Children with Autism Spectrum Disorders

Kirby Lentz, Ed.D.

APC

Autism Asperger Publishing Company
P.O. Box 23173
Shawnee Mission, KS 66283-0173
www.asperger.net

© 2004 by Autism Asperger Publishing Company
P.O. Box 23173
Shawnee Mission, KS 66283-0173
www.asperger.net

Publisher's Cataloging-in-Publication
(Provided by Quality Books, Inc.)

Lentz, Kirby.
    Hopes and dreams : an IEP guide for parents of
children with autism spectrum disorders / Kirby Lentz.
    p. cm.
    Includes bibliographical references.
    ISBN 1-931282-66-8
    LCCN 2004114443

    1. Autistic children--Education. 2. Individualized
instruction. 3. Education--Parent participation.
I. Title.

LC4717.5.L46 2004   371.94
                    QBI04-200460

This book is designed in Amigo and Helvetica Neue

Managing Editor: Kirsten McBride
Editorial Support: Ginny Biddulph

Printed in the United States of America

This guide is dedicated to
students and adults who in their
own way share their hopes
and dreams with the world so
the world may understand.

Acknowledgments

I would like to extend my appreciation to all the families, parents, and students who have worked to improve their participation in the IEP process, and the teachers who have been receptive to new ideas and care deeply about the education of students with autism spectrum disorders.

A heartfelt gratitude is extended to B. J., my wife, who encouraged "us" to complete this project and gave me the confidence to share these ideas. I greatly appreciate the hours she spent reading and rereading this book as a parent would read it, and sharing her thoughts and ideas of how to improve it.

I am most grateful to Kirsten McBride, managing editor, who worked so patiently with me and provided so competently ideas and perspectives to make this manual understandable and more readable.

Further, this guide would not have been possible without the feedback provided by teachers and parents, and without the expertise and willingness of the following peer reviewers: Norma Schlicht, Vicky Shanley, and Robin Hansen, parents; Laurie Enos, psychologist; Pam Foegen, program specialist; and Julie Simonson, special education teacher.

A special thank-you is expressed to Diane Hietpas, director of special education at Chileda Institute, La Crosse, Wisconsin, for her expert assistance in preparing this manuscript.

Finally, I sincerely appreciate the support, love and interest expressed by my mother, Marjorie Lentz, and my mother-in-law, Helen Wall. In many ways they have taught me to do the best you can do and care about people.

Contents

HOW TO USE THIS GUIDE

This guide is written primarily for parents, but teachers and other school personnel will find it informative and practical as well. The goal is to help build a relationship between teachers and parents by sharing relevant and meaningful information not only to construct an effective individualized education program (IEP), but to collaborate across home, school, and the community for the life span success of students with autism spectrum disorders.

This process involves a significant amount of work. Parents are encouraged to read one chapter at a time and complete the worksheet(s) included at the end of most chapters. Take some time between chapters to let it all sink in. The work you do for each chapter will be more meaningful this way. In short, do not expect to be able to read this guide in its entirety in one sitting.

The worksheets are especially important as they provide an opportunity to decide on the direction you feel is most beneficial for you and your child in a given area. The thinking you do here reflects the hopes and dreams for you and your

The goal is to help build a relationship between teachers and parents . . .

child. Parents are encouraged to share what they have learned from this book with teachers and other school professionals working with their child.

Teachers and other school personnel, in turn, are encouraged to follow the same steps as outlined for parents. Even though "parent" is referenced throughout, often "parent" can be changed to "teacher" without otherwise changing the meaning. Teachers may want to share the ideas presented here with the parents of their students.

An extra set of all worksheets may be found in the back of the guide. Owners of this book have permission to copy these pages for their own use. For your convenience, blank worksheets are also included on the enclosed CD.

Enjoy, and achieve your hopes and dreams as well as those of your child.

– Kirby Lentz

Chapter 1

LET'S GO TO WORK

I nstead of hiding the disclaimer somewhere in small print, I want to emphasize from the beginning: I am not an attorney, and this book has nothing to do with the legalities or interpretation of special education law. There are tons of books, guides, and briefs that address the Individuals with Disabilities Education Act (IDEA) and its most recent upgrade, the reauthorization of IDEA of 1997.

One of the hopes behind this guide is to avert the legal stuff. Thus, the underlying contention is that if parents of children with an autism spectrum disorder (ASD) work cooperatively and collaboratively with teachers and schools, legal action and subsequent litigation in most cases will not be necessary. This theory is simple: If parents and teachers work together, the student with an ASD is afforded an IEP that has a good chance of success. If, on the other hand, problems evolve between parents and teachers, the impartial hearing officer makes a few bucks, and the parent, teacher, and student all lose.

Every parent with a child with an ASD as well as parents of adult children with ASD will find this guide useful, as it will

FLASHPOINTS:

✔ Parents are equal partners on the IEP team

✔ Collaboration with the school is essential

✔ Hopes and Dreams Worksheet: *Getting Organized*

help them to better support and advocate for their child. By reading this guide, parents will learn how to participate more effectively in IEP meetings and become familiar with what information is important to present to the IEP team.

Parents of adult children will need to replace "IEP" with the acronym used in the various settings where their son or daughter is receiving services, such as IPP (Individual Program Plan), ITP (Individual Training Plan), ISP (Individual Service Plan), and similar terms. The key to supporting adult children with ASD is for parents to stay involved with their adult child's program. As their child reaches adulthood, many parents begin to withdraw from the active involvement they may have engaged in while the child was in school. There is a tendency among many to think that adult children must learn to find their own way and become independent. While I firmly believe in encouraging and fostering independence to the greatest extent possible, I encourage all parents to remain active in their adult child's life and program planning.

Active parent participation is critical at any age. The Hopes and Dreams model will provide you with a new way of thinking about the educational process and a new way of interacting and advocating for your child with ASD. I have talked with many parents who are frustrated with the system and feel they do not understand how the system works. Thus, unfortunately, many parents resort to legal action, viewing it as the only avenue left to ensure their child can progress educationally. Many teachers and administrators, on the other hand, feel that the parents always hold the trump card and that they have no other recourse than to abide by the rules, go through the steps, and make sure all the paperwork is completed and submitted on time.

I have sat on both ends of the table. In my professional life I chair IEP meetings and conferences for students with ASD. In that role, sadly, I have seen and been responsible for parents feeling frustrated, angry, bewildered, and nervous about sitting around a table discussing every imaginable aspect of their child's life. In my role as a parent, I have also sat in IEP meetings and conferences feeling outnumbered and confused as teachers and other school professionals tried to tell me things I knew and things I did not know about my child.

It was not until I experienced being a parent during a school conference that I understood what the IEP process was supposed to be. The IEP process is an opportunity for parents and teachers to sit down, whenever possible with the student, to discuss the hopes and dreams that parents have for their child, teachers have for their student, and the student has for his or her life.

The chapters in this book follow a deliberate sequence starting with thinking about parenting a child with disabilities. Then we will try to understand what teachers think. After a brief introduction to the IEP process and evaluations, the Hopes and Dreams model will be presented. By walking through the six steps that make up the model, parents will gain a new understanding of how to be active participants and equal partners with the school. Then the actual IEP meeting will be discussed, and hints for active participation and equal partnership will be offered. Chapter 9 looks at transition and life after the school years, an area that is often overlooked. Finally, the epilogue, "Hopes and Dreams," encourages us all to advocate so our children will learn to advocate for themselves to the greatest extent possible.

The outcome of the process outlined in this guide is an IEP that meets the hopes and dreams of parents, children, and teachers. To collaboratively develop this thing we call the IEP, we all have to do our part. This guide was written to help you do your part. After reading the ideas presented here, one mother wrote, "I shared your forms with the teacher after my husband and I filled them out. This was the first time I ever felt we developed the IEP together."

The following worksheet, *Getting Organized*, not only encourages you to put all forms, evaluations, reports, and IEPs in a workable filing system, it also helps you get ready for the Hopes and Dreams model process. The worksheet is

The outcome of the process outlined in this guide is an IEP that meets the hopes and dreams of parents, children, and teachers

simply a check-off system. A portable file box purchased at any office supply or discount store will work perfectly. When you have that pile of papers filed in a file box in chronological order – from most recent to last – just check off the item(s) as they are completed along the way.

HOPES AND DREAMS WORKSHEET
Getting Organized

✔	File Topics	Filed (date)
	Notices of IEP team meetings	
	School evaluation reports	
	Determination manifestation (eligibility)	
	File for initial IEP with progress summaries	
	File(s) for each successive IEP with progress summaries (Keep three years' worth of IEP updates and other supporting IEP materials until a three-year reevaluation is completed. Then start a new three-year cycle.)	
	Copies of Hopes and Dreams worksheets each time completed	
	Copies of any related medical evaluations and reports	
	Copies of any related professional evaluations and reports	
	Behavioral notes	
	Progress notes of significant and not-so-significant events you feel are special and noteworthy	
	Selected photographs or other materials you feel demonstrate success	

Chapter 2

WHAT WE HAVE LEARNED FROM PARENTS

How do you feel about being a parent of a child with an ASD? This is a question you will have to think about before going much further. Some parents find this question difficult to answer, others find it easy. And some don't want to think about it at all.

The question can probably never be fully answered; it will be a sort of answer-in-progress. Nevertheless, think about it! The answers that pop into your head are not important in and of themselves, but the process of "thinking about what we think" is important because it helps to frame attitudes and values that are important to us. Thoughts such as feeling overwhelmed, frustrated, challenged, uninformed, once identified, lead parents to view a larger picture of their child. This picture includes thinking of your child in school, at home, in the community, as a teenager or adult, and with other people.

As you begin to think about feeling overwhelmed, for example, the process of thinking in a larger picture may help you start thinking of a way to learn more about autism, asking for help when necessary, or finding out about support groups and home interventions. Simply put, we need to understand

FLASHPOINTS:

✔ Understanding attitudes about parenting a child with ASD

✔ What other parents feel is important and frustrating

✔ Hopes and Dreams Worksheet: *How Do You Feel about Parenting Your Child with ASD?*

our emotions and attitudes to gain a clearer understanding of what is important – now and for the future.

To help parents think about being a parent of a child with ASD, I typically ask four questions. Interestingly, parents' answers do not differ greatly among themselves and – as we will see in Chapter 3 – they don't differ greatly from those of teachers and other school personnel.

A few years ago, my wife and I spent nearly three weeks in South India meeting parents of children with ASD and other disabilities. Surprisingly, their responses were very similar to responses I have heard in this country – despite the enormous differences between the two countries. For example, there is little, if any, public education for children with disabilities in India, and many children with disabilities receive educational services only through privately funded and charitable schools.

To give you an idea of what parents' responses are typically like, let's look at each of the four questions and representative answers. The four questions were asked of parents during small discussion groups during workshops and conferences.

1. *What has been the most difficult or frustrating issue you have faced as a parent of a child with autism spectrum disorders?*

   • Overwhelming; do not know where to start

   • Little or no awareness in our society about autism (#1 response in both India and the United States)

   • Dealing with family members who do not understand

   • Finding doctors who know something about autism

   • Uninformed teachers or teachers not willing to learn about autism spectrum disorders

- Teaching abstract concepts to our child

- Child's inability to communicate with parents and others

- Teaching toileting skills

- Dealing with adolescents as their body changes and matures

- Failure of schools to communicate clearly and frequently

- No assessment of how well the system works (including education, medical, social services)

- Discipline

- Keeping the family system "normal"

- Accepting that your child is not "normal"

- Inclusion

- Being patient with the child

- Understanding the child's wants and needs

- Having a normal child locked inside whom we cannot reach

- Knowing our child's disabilities and sensory needs and seeing the struggle, but having the community see them as bad and poorly behaved children, and parents as irresponsible

- Behaviors; how to cope with behaviors at home, school, and community

- Fear

- Not knowing what to do

- Parents and educators not getting valuable information

Interestingly, parents' answers do not differ greatly among themselves and they don't differ greatly from those of teachers and other school personnel.

2. What has been your most successful accomplishment or experience as a parent of a child with an autism spectrum disorder?

- The TEACCH program

- Picture Exchange Communication System (PECS)

- Being able to function day-to-day as a family

- Getting the school district to move one step at a time

- My son developing eye contact

- Charts at home outlining expectations

- Open communication with school personnel

- Looking at and accepting the "little gains" vs. the "big picture"

- Siblings becoming more accepting of the child with autism

- Inclusion

- Parent networking

- Having a deep love and understanding of my child

- Teachers who have a good insight and work with students knowing they can do the work

- Good teachers and schools

- Early intervention

- Connecting with families and support groups

- Devoted therapists and professionals

- No dairy or grains in the diet

- Vitamins

3. What is missing?

- Educating teachers about autism spectrum disorders

- Better parent-teacher communication

- Service supports like respite care, child-sitting

- Information about services

- Getting a diagnosis

- After getting a diagnosis, getting information on options

- Information at point of first diagnosis

- Public awareness and acceptance

- Special education tailored to the specific child

- Stronger advocacy

- Parent networking

- More research

- Daycare for children ages 12 to 18

- Doctors having knowledge about autism

- Summer school

- Community recreation opportunities

- Plans for continued care and love after we are gone

There are no right or wrong answers to the four questions. The answers given here are merely intended to serve as a way to start thinking about how you feel.

4. What ideas do you have to do things differently?

- Training for all educators

- System to coordinate 6-7 teachers at middle school

- Better way to present first diagnosis to parents

- Diagnosis to help parents move forward and eliminate other possibilities

- Better access to resources

- Allowing parents to follow their instincts, not having to wait for professional recommendations and the schools to prepare an IEP

- Focus on helpful research

- Financial compensation for teachers to learn more about autism

- Autism to be part of teacher preparation in college

- A case manager to coordinate all services like respite, occupational therapy, school, doctors

- More child advocates: family, teachers, church, and society

- Parent training

- Consultant to visit homes and classrooms and explain what is going on

There are no right or wrong answers to the four questions. The answers given here are merely intended to serve as a way to start thinking about how you feel.

One parent wrote, "After listing all the bad feelings I had about being a parent of a boy with ASD, I began to realize I was so fortunate because I now really appreciated all the little things in life I previously overlooked." In reference to poor school-home communication, another parent reported, "When I thought about this some more, I knew I could do something. I started passing ideas and new things my son was doing at home to the teacher by jotting down little notes. About a week later the teacher started doing the same." Yet another parent wrote about the suggestion that we think about how we feel, "Guess I'll have to do that!"

While it is not possible to draw any specific conclusions from parents' responses to the four questions, it is easy to see that there are many important issues affecting parents. Issues of first diagnosis, parent-teacher communications, public awareness, and knowledgeable professionals are well documented. The only conclusions that are meaningful, however, are the ones that each parent identifies for his or her unique situation.

Sometimes thinking about how we feel about parenting a child with an ASD will lead to new ideas, sometimes an initiative to better serve children – and almost every time a sense of peace and connectedness. Even though parents have extraordinary responsibilities when their child has an ASD, when they are connected to their thinking, parents' feelings, beliefs, and values are more grounded. The same goes for the whole family.

How do you feel about your child with ASD? Are there things other parents have said that make sense to you, that you disagree with, or that they have missed? What we have learned from parents should start you on your thinking journey. You will probably never complete this task. You will find yourself modifying and adapting your thoughts as you go along.

The following worksheet will help parents analyze their emotions and attitudes in an effort to develop an understanding of parenting a child with ASD. This understanding, in turn, will help drive a collaborative process that will result in a useful plan to meet child and family needs at home, in school, and throughout the community.

You will note that a fifth question has been added to the worksheet. This question is very important. While you may be thinking that you have no time left for yourself once you have taken care of everybody else's needs, it is essential that you somehow dedicate some time to you.

. . . when they are connected to their thinking, parents' feelings, beliefs, and values are more grounded. The same goes for the whole family.

HOPES AND DREAMS WORKSHEET
How Do You Feel about Parenting Your Child with ASD?

Directions: Write your thoughts for each question.

1. What has been the most difficult or frustrating issue you have faced as a parent of a child with autism spectrum disorders?

2. What has been your most successful accomplishment or experience as a parent of a child with an autism spectrum disorder?

3. What is missing?

4. What ideas do you have to do things differently?

5. What do you do for yourself to relieve stress or to relax?

Chapter 3

WHAT WE HAVE LEARNED FROM TEACHERS

Asking teachers what they think about students with ASD is also important. Responses from the teachers are as necessary for parents to hear as it is for teachers to hear parents' concerns and thoughts. Yet, as mentioned, often parents and teachers share the same concerns and feelings. The Hopes and Dreams model is built on a process of collaboration. Sharing concerns and thoughts develops the beginning of a meaningful relationship.

After one of my presentations a father came up to me and said, "When you talked about sharing feelings, I did just that. I told my son's teacher at a conference that I was frustrated because I couldn't find good information about Asperger Syndrome and that I had been looking without success for other families dealing with the same thing. The teacher laughed and said that he was also looking for resources and for training; besides, he was looking for a local expert to help him in the classroom." They ended up sharing information and, through a contact the teacher made, they found another family with a child with Asperger Syndrome, and all got together and helped each other out.

FLASHPOINTS:

✔ How teachers feel about teaching a student with ASD

✔ Parents and teachers may see things about the same way

✔ Hopes and Dreams Worksheet: *Parent-Teacher Communication*

I have asked teachers and school personnel to answer essentially the same questions as those asked of parents and reported in Chapter 2. Not as many teachers were involved in the survey, but their responses appear consistent and are insightful as you will note below.

1. *What has been most frustrating to you as a teacher of a child with autism spectrum disorders?*

   - Lack of communication between parents and teachers

   - No time to talk with parents

   - No time to set up individual schedules

   - No time to try new things and maintain existing classroom activities

   - Little time to get to know the child as an individual

   - Little information on the first day of school; not knowing what to do

   - Parents forgetting they are the real experts

   - Trying to maintain a safe environment for all students, aides, and teachers

   - Lack of time to set up adequate activities and experiences

   - Paperwork and documentation seemingly more important than teaching

   - Dealing with aggressive and self-injurious behaviors

2. *What has been most helpful to you and your students with autism spectrum disorders?*

   - Parents giving information about the child outside of the school day

   - Routine scheduling to communicate with others and parents

- TEACCH and visual schedules

- Administrators who understand the amount of time necessary to work effectively with students with ASD

- Autism training opportunities

- Working with other professionals who have knowledge about autism

3. **What's missing in the service system?**

- Team approach to planning curriculum

- Time, time, time

- More speech therapy time in the classroom so teachers can grasp what they are doing

- Not isolating the "specials" (speech, OT, PT, adapted phys. ed.)

- Fewer "pull-out" times

- Home and community opportunities to help build on educational objectives

- Case coordination

4. **What would be helpful to you and other teachers of children with autism spectrum disorders?**

- Time to reflect on the day and everything that went on; time to share ideas; time to prepare meaningful activities; time to research new methods; time to share concepts with others; time to get to know the students; time to work with parents

- Opportunities to receive strategy training

- Team work and team problem solving

Both teachers and parents agree that there is little time to do what each would like to do.

Thinking about what is important to the teacher and how the teacher thinks about students with ASD is important by adding another dimension to parents' thinking. As parents begin to share their thoughts with teachers, and teachers share their thoughts with parents, it is surprising to learn that their lists do not differ greatly.

Both teachers and parents agree that there is little time to do what each would like to do. Likewise, parents often list that "teachers have too much paperwork," whereas teachers respond, "paperwork requirements takes too much time away from face-to-face instruction." One hypothesized, and very unscientific, conclusion is that parents' and teachers' "I wish that could happen" lists would be very similar – to the point that they could be collapsed into a "We wish that …" list. Unfortunately, when parents and teachers do not share concerns, the reality is usually quite the opposite. Parents have difficulty understanding the constraints of the teacher, and teachers do not understand why parents seem so demanding or are so unrealistic.

Generally, I believe most parents and most teachers have the same common goal – working to make the "I wish that …" list possible. But problems arise due to the different perceptions, or environments, of parents and teachers. Consider the following:

- Parents see school as one third of the day, *whereas*

  … Teachers see school as 100% of their time with the student.

- Parents understand the circles of interaction with family, friends, and community, *whereas*

  … Teachers see influences from the other services, speech and language, occupational therapy, behavior management.

- Parents fear the uncertainty of weekends, holidays and summer, *whereas*

  … Teachers seek the rejuvenation of weekends, holidays, and summer.

- Parents look at the IEP as a statement of hope, *whereas*

  … Teachers see the IEP as something they have to complete within mandated timeframes and with federally required content.

Does that mean that these differences in perception and environment between parents and teachers will stand in the way of accomplishing what we have been talking about – coming together on behalf of the child with ASD? Hopefully not. But to make sure it doesn't, you will have to play a more active role in your child's education than many parents are used to.

In Chapter 6 you will learn how to coordinate the environment in such a way that perceptions of the IEP or the environment do not block your way. The IEP as a document is:

- either loved or hated by parents

- either seen as time-consuming or controlling by teachers

- either feared or forgotten by school district administrators

- either used as a regulating or a funding vehicle by state departments

These different perceptions of the IEP will not go away, but by following the suggestions and strategies presented in this book, you and your child's teachers can use the IEP environment as an effective tool to work jointly on behalf of your child instead of seeing it as a source of conflict.

Many parents find themselves in an uncomfortable position when advocating for their child. Don't be too forceful or too meek. Advocating for your child is different from fighting with the school district, on the one hand, and allowing school personnel to direct the entire IEP and the related services your child receives, on the other. At some point you and the school will be together for a placement meeting, an IEP meeting, or a parent-teacher conference. To be better

. . . you will have to play a more active role in your child's education than many parents are used to.

prepared, understand the environmental differences and the similarities of the "I wish that ..." list.

If your child has only recently been diagnosed, you may not yet have experienced any aspect of the IEP process and the related meetings. Therefore, the "I wish that ..." list and the environmental differences mentioned above may not make much sense to you now. But try to put yourself in the shoes of your child's teacher or other school staff members to gain an understanding of their perspectives. It is far too common for a parent to show up at an IEP meeting with an attorney or an advocate with a demand list designed to force the school, the teacher, or both, to meet the dictum for services. While the dictum approach may produce some immediate results, it will have a negative impact on future meetings. I have been involved in meetings in which the advocate and a teacher were downright nasty and, as a result, the entire IEP team soon shut down. I never saw the resulting IEP, but the planning process was destroyed. The goal for parent and teacher interactions must be collaboration, with each advocating for the child and the student, but with one sight in mind – a functional and meaningful IEP.

In all the most important areas, you and the teacher will think more alike than differently, as evidenced by the similarities in the responses from the teachers and the parents to the four questions listed earlier. Based on these shared goals, you may wish to think about the following question:

> "What would happen if I, the parent, and the teacher put our heads together and discussed the things we thought were most important?"

… Do not ask this question yet. Wait until the IEP meeting or some time after that, but start thinking about what you might say.

What have we learned from teachers? Briefly, we have learned that parents and teachers learn from each other, and that they generally share the same goals for the child.

Continue your thinking journey. Think about the worksheet on the following page and complete it as soon after reading this chapter as possible.

This exercise gets you started to identify important issues necessary for developing your thoughts for a collaborative IEP, and processing your hopes and dreams for your child.

The goal for parent and teacher interactions must be collaboration, with each advocating for the child and the student.

HOPES AND DREAMS WORKSHEET
Parent-Teacher Communication

Directions: Write down your thoughts. You will not need to share this with anyone. Refer to it frequently and revise it as necessary. Review it prior to any meeting with your child's teacher(s).

What are my hopes and dreams for my child?

Am I comfortable sharing my hopes and dreams with my child's teacher? If not, why?

My "short list" of concerns (I need to start a little slow at this point).

My "short list" of what I wish would happen (I do not have to go overboard here as I want to build a better relationship with the teacher).

Some issues are not the school's responsibility. Which ones?

If the teacher and I could work on something together, what would it be?

Chapter 4

WHAT IS AN IEP AND WHERE DID IT COME FROM?

The IEP came about when P. L. 94-142, the Education of All Handicapped Children Act, was ratified by Congress in 1975 and signed into law. Since that time the act has been reauthorized several times, most recently in 1997 when the Individuals with Disabilities Education Act (IDEA) was passed. At each reauthorization, modifications have been proposed to make the law more current and "better."

Even though the IEP has withstood each reauthorization and continuing scrutiny by legislators – who may not have a keen sense of special education, let alone disabilities – it remains a fragile instrument. The IEP is fragile because, although its alleged purpose – to provide an individualized and appropriate educational plan – is well conceived, its actual use often seems questionable.

After nearly two and a half decades, one would think the IEP could stand alone, guiding the provision of special education services to children with exceptional education needs. Instead, it has primarily become a legal instrument. Yet, it still remains an instrument that plans for the individual provision of special education and related services for students requiring that such a document be written and

FLASHPOINTS:

✔ **The IEP is a great tool**

✔ **Equal parent participation depends on preparedness**

✔ **Why a review of past team meetings is so important**

✔ **Hopes and Dreams Worksheet:** *Memories of Past IEP Team Meetings* filed as a way of summarizing evaluations and documenting disability classification.

As originally framed in P. L. 94-142, the IEP was probably the best conceived educational planning device ever devised. Specifically, it included reasonable methods for disability classification, monitoring of progress, and identification of areas in need of revision. All of this was based on the identified needs of each individual special education student.

The IEP was intended to be a team-directed plan constructed by parents, students, and special as well as general education teachers. The 1997 IDEA added an administrator to the team, and now requires that all participants be equal partners in decision making.

That's good, but how many parents feel they have an equal status during the conference?

The reason why many parents feel they do not have equal say during an IEP meeting or conference is that they often do not know what to say. They do not know what is important and what is not important, what the protocol is, what the rules are, and so on. Sure, every parent receives a flyer from the district explaining due process and parent rights, but due process is exactly what we want to avoid. Many parents would feel less intimidated and uncomfortable attending IEP meetings if they were better prepared.

By doing their homework as outlined in this book, parents can make a positive change. It is not essential to be experts on interpreting the IDEA to understand protocol and meeting agendas, or even to be acutely aware of the technicalities of the regulations of the IEP. That's the job of the school. Parents' responsibility is to be prepared to present what is going on with their child.

In Chapter 6 we will go through the procedures necessary to prepare for the meeting. After completing the steps outlined, parents will be able to provide meaningful and helpful information to the school, including:

1. What's important for the child

2. Strengths and needs as seen by the parents in environments other than school

3. What interests the child has

4. What interventions and strategies have been successful in the past

5. What will be helpful in the future

It is better if the child can self-report this information to the IEP team. Whenever possible, parents and teachers should help the child/student to prepare for the IEP meeting. With appropriate supports such as notes or verbal cues, parents or teachers can assist the child in relating the above information in some fashion during the team meeting.

If you have been through the process before, you know that usually all teachers and other school professionals (speech pathologists, occupational therapists, etc.) have done their homework prior to an IEP meeting. For example, their evaluations represent current testing or assessments, and relevant recommendations and summaries are attached.

Parents also have to be prepared. If parents do their homework prior to the IEP meeting, issues that are impeding or have previously impeded parent participation will be eliminated or at least greatly minimized. Your participation is important. The school staff who are attempting to write the best possible IEP for your child will appreciate and value your input and your efforts to work collaboratively with the school. It beats due process and is cheaper than litigation, and – most important – is best for the child!

As you prepare to complete the *Memories of Past IEP Meetings* worksheet on the next page, try to remember when you felt uncomfortable and why, as well as when you thought things were going well. This exercise will help you identify times and topics you may wish to become more or less engaged in at the IEP team meetings. If you are a "new" parent, you will find it helpful to read through and think about the questions and possible answers too.

> If parents do their homework prior to the IEP meeting, issues that are impeding or have previously impeded parent participation will be eliminated or at least greatly minimized.

HOPES AND DREAMS WORKSHEET
Memories of Past IEP Meetings

Directions: Think about previous IEP meetings you have attended and answer the questions below. If you have never attended an IEP meeting, review the questions anyway and try to imagine how you may feel.

What did I like about some of the IEP meetings?

How did I feel before and during the meetings?

What made me feel uncomfortable?

When was my input requested?

What contributions did I make at the meeting?

Did I feel good about the outcome?

Did I feel the needs of my child were met?

How could the meeting have been different?

How could I have been more helpful as the parent expert?

Chapter 5

INTRODUCTION TO SCHOOL EVALUATIONS AND ASSESSMENTS

School evaluations and assessments are important, and required, components of special education law to ensure the best possible program is developed to meet the child's unique needs. However, for many parents school evaluations produce a great deal of unease, often because they do not fully understand the nature or purpose of evaluation in general, and individual instruments in particular.

This chapter is not meant to provide a full explanation of evaluation procedures, administration, or interpretation. Instead, the intent is to help parents understand the role of evaluations in developing the IEP and subsequently their child's instructional program.

One of the most misunderstood aspects of the special education process for parents is the evaluation. Many parents voice concerns about evaluation results, are not sure how they are determined, and question how they are used. When a child with ASD is evaluated, test results often do not paint a clear or accurate picture of the child's ability or prognosis for future learning. Thus, parents with children with ASD often cite the following as concerns about evaluations:

FLASHPOINTS:

✔ **Types of educational evaluations**

✔ **Parent/guardian consent for conducting evaluations**

✔ **How evaluation results are used**

✔ **Common questions about evaluations**

✔ **Hopes and Dreams Worksheet:** *Summary of Evaluation Recommendations*

1. Sometimes children with ASD have splinter skills: skills that are acquired or learned out of the typical learning sequences; for example, some children are able to spell words far above their reading level. Often evaluation protocols do not accurately reflect a score consistent with the child's ability.

2. When tests are administered by unknown persons in unfamiliar environments, the child's performance may not be authentically measured.

3. Results may be negatively impacted by testing parameters such as time limitations or confusing directions.

4. Evaluation results are reported at IEP team meetings with a lot of numbers that have little to do with what the child can do in real life, or results are not connected to educational planning.

In short, evaluations are a cause of concern to many parents, and the results are easily misunderstood.

In the case of ASD, many times the child's physician makes the initial or first diagnosis. Prior to the first diagnosis, most parents report that they thought their child's development was not proceeding at a typical rate and therefore took the child to their family physician. When physicians suspect ASD, they may recommend a referral for further testing and evaluation by a developmental psychologist or staff at the local school district.

As schools have a responsibility to identify children with disabilities in their district prior to their enrollment in kindergarten, parents should report to the district if they believe their child has an ASD. When this happens, generally, a school psychologist and other members of the school staff, such as a speech and language pathologist, or an occupational therapist, evaluate the child. An initial IEP team is then put together, consisting of the staff members conducting evaluations, a director of special education or pupil services, the parents, and perhaps a teacher from the appropriate grade level. This team, including the parents, will meet to arrive at (a) a confirming diagnosis of an autism spectrum disorder or a diagnosis of another disability, or (b) a determination that the child has no known disability based upon the eligibility criteria established by the state.

Evaluations are a part of every IEP and every placement decision. Furthermore, evaluations are a necessary element in determining the need for special education services, which must be re-assessed every three years while the child is in school.

Evaluations are a part of every IEP and every placement decision.

In the following, we will start by briefly reviewing why evaluations are conducted and how they are used in the IEP process. Additionally, several ideas will be presented for parents to think about.

Types of Testing Instruments

Generally, school evaluations fall into two categories of instruments or tests, norm-referenced and criterion-referenced. Both are widely used in all areas of education to determine eligibility for special education, to measure academic performance, to decide category of disability (such as autism, mental retardation, emotional/behavioral disability, etc.), to assess adaptive skills, and to develop IEPs and educational services.

Norm-Referenced Instruments

Norm-referenced instruments are mostly used to identify and verify eligibility for special education services and to demonstrate progress in academic achievement. By their nature, norm-referenced tests are given to large numbers of students, and from the scores of all the test-takers, statisticians determine a standard or norm for which test scores fall into an average, below-average, or above-average range.

Norm-referenced evaluation instruments are classified as either (a) intelligence and diagnostic screening instruments or (b) academic and achievement tests. In the special education process, the diagnostic or screening tests are often used to determine eligibility for special education services.

Diagnostic and screening instruments.

A good example of diagnostic and screening instrument is the IQ test. Tests like the Leiter International Performance Scale-Revised (Roid & Miller, 1997) or the Wechsler Intelligence Scale for Children, Revised (WISC-IV) (Psychological Corporation, 2003) are used to measure intelligence by comparing an individual child to a sample of children from across the country.

Examples of diagnostic screening instruments of particular interest to parents of children with ASD include the Gilliam Autism Rating Scale (Gilliam, 1999), Autism Screening Instrument for Educational Planning (Krug, Arick, & Almond, 1993), and the Asperger Syndrome Diagnostic Scale (Myles, Bock, & Simpson, 2001).

To yield valid and reliable results, norm-referenced instruments usually must be completed within certain timelines using specified testing conditions. Therefore, these instruments have a detailed protocol for use by trained examiners.

Academic and achievement instruments.

The second type of norm-referenced tests, achievement and academic skills instruments, are often administered on a yearly basis for students receiving special education services. In many cases such testing occurs just prior to the annual IEP meeting to:

1. review the past year's accomplishments

2. update the results in the Present Levels of Educational Performance section of the IEP

3. develop a planning strategy for the upcoming year.

Examples of norm-referenced achievement instruments include the Receptive One-Word Picture Vocabulary Test (Brownwell, 2000), Brigance Diagnostic Comprehensive Inventory of Basic Skills (Brigance, 1999), Kaufman Test of Educational Achievement (Kaufman & Kaufman, 1985), and the Iowa Tests of Basic Skills (Hoover, Hieronymus, Frisbie, & Dunbar, 1996). Many others are also frequently used. Besides, there are numerous tests of specific academic areas such as reading, mathematics, literacy, and oral and perceptual motor skills.

A sensory profile is another type of norm-referenced assessment instrument that is often used when children with ASD display hyper- or hypo-sensitivity to sensory stimuli, such as touch, proximity to others, auditory and visual presentations, and responses to light and environmental sounds. Usually administered by an occupational therapist, a sensory profile records typical and non-typical responses to an array of sensory presentations.

Similar to other norm-referenced evaluations, sensory assessments are compared to a sample population to determine if an individual response is or is not within "normal" ranges. Thus, sensory profiles are intended to indicate the existence of any widely different responses than would be typically expected. One commonly used sensory assessment is the Sensory Profile (Dunn, 1999).

> . . . criterion-referenced instruments compare student responses against specific tasks or other criteria such as a school curriculum or established standards of learning.

Criterion-Referenced Instruments

As opposed to norm-references instruments, criterion-referenced instruments are based on specific educational outcomes or skills and are designed to determine whether a student is meeting an established criterion. That is, rather than comparing a child's scores with those of others as is the case on norm-referenced instruments, criterion-referenced instruments compare student responses against specific tasks or other criteria such as a school curriculum or established standards of learning. These criteria are often unique to a given state or even an individual school district.

Scoring of criterion-referenced instruments can involve checking statements such as "can do/cannot do," "pass/fail," or "yes/no." Scores are compared to the specific skill or criterion specified by the instrument. An example would be a spelling test in which the student is asked to spell a word from a verbal request or a math test where the student has to complete a math problem. Once the student has completed the assignment, the teacher checks whether the answer is correct or incorrect.

Commonly used criterion-referenced instruments include the Vineland Adaptive Behavior Scale (Harrison, 1985), the Adaptive Behavior Scale-School Revised 2 (Lambert, Nihira, & Leland, 1993), and Scales of Independent Behavior-Revised (Bruininks, Woodcock, Weatherman, & Hill, 1996). Numerous criterion-referenced instruments are available that may provide valuable data to determine educational strategies and planning.

Behavior checklists.

A common form of criterion-referenced instrument, behavior checklists, consists of listings of skills and behaviors organized into developmental areas or domains. For example, the Adaptive Behavior Scale-School, 2nd Edition (Lambert et al., 1993), assesses 16 domains in two parts:

Part I	Part II
I. Independent Functioning	X. Social Behavior
II. Physical Development	XI. Conformity
III. Economic Activity	XII. Trustworthiness
IV. Language Development	XIII. Stereotyped and Hyperactive Behavior
V. Numbers and Time	
VI. Prevocational / Vocational Activity	XIV. Self-Abusive Behaviors
	XV. Social Engagement
VII. Self-Direction	XVI. Disturbing Interpersonal Behavior
VIII. Responsibility	
IX. Socialization	

Each domain lists a series of skills roughly aligned with typical development. For example, a domain area such as Socialization (Domain IX) lists in developmental order several benchmark skills as illustrated below.

Domain IX. Socialization

Cooperation (circle the highest level – point value for area of cooperation)

Offers assistance to others	2
Is willing to help if asked	1
Never helps others	0

Consideration for Others	Yes	No
Shows interest in the affairs of others	1	0
Takes care of others' belongings	1	0
Directs or manages the affairs of others when needed	1	0
Shows consideration of others' feelings	1	0

Parents are often asked to complete adaptive behavior checklists or to do so in concert with a teacher familiar with the assessment and the scoring procedures. The evaluator (parent or teacher, etc.) simply identifies the skill level on the checklist at which the child demonstrates consistent ability.

After the assessments are completed, a teacher or psychologist scores the responses, usually by adding the number of points under each domain. This results in a "raw score." The raw score is compared to a statistical chart in the test manual to arrive at a standard score, and sometimes age and grade equivalencies as well. Finally, the scores may be placed on a graph or a score sheet to more clearly identify areas of strengths and weaknesses for the individual child, not in comparison to a sample of similar-aged children as is the case with norm-referenced tests.

Criterion-referenced instruments are a widely used way to determine the specific skills a child is able to perform based

Parents are often asked to complete adaptive behavior checklists or to do so in concert with a teacher . . .

upon a set of standards or a given curriculum. As such, these instruments can pinpoint areas that need specialized or additional instruction either to support the work of teachers/parents or to include formally in the IEP team process.

Modifications and Accommodations

For many students, especially students with ASD, it is valuable to know if special modifications are being applied to the testing protocol. This includes extended time limits, use of computer or a scribe, an area free of distractions and noise where students can take the test, and so on. If special modifications or accommodations have not been made for your child and you think they are warranted, you may wish to talk to school personnel about modifications that may produce more accurate results without contaminating the evaluative data.

In one case a psychologist came into the classroom and practiced activities similar to those found in an upcoming assessment with the child to be evaluated several times prior to the actual testing. This was not done purely to attain a good score, but to help familiarize the student with the evaluator and the types of tasks she would be required to do during the actual testing.

Some would claim that such preparation destroys the validity of the testing instrument. However, in many cases the test administrator feels that it leads to a more accurate description of the child's ability than if the student comes in cold and is confronted by an unfamiliar person. In a similar effort to arrive at a true measure, speech, physical, and occupational therapists sometimes take several weeks to conduct an assessment, knowing that various locations and different days will produce a variety of responses. The goal is to find a way to arrive at the most accurate results possible.

Accurate results will yield a clear idea of:

1. teaching strategies to be used

2. meaningful objectives and goals for a given student

3. correct category for eligibility or continued special educational services

4. appropriate educational placement

Evaluation Results

After the assessments are completed, the evaluation results are reported at the IEP team meeting when the team determines and writes the Present Level of Educational Performance section of the IEP. The evaluator discusses both the child's strengths and areas where the child is in need of educational intervention. As mentioned earlier, both norm-referenced and criterion-referenced instruments are used, producing scores in comparison either to others (norm-referenced) or to target goals or skills (criterion-referenced). Most of the time such scores are expressed as a percentile or age or grade equivalencies.

It is generally accepted that percentile scores and standard scores provide the most meaningful evaluation results. Age and grade equivalencies, by contrast, can be misleading and may be misunderstood. Knowing that your child scored at a three-year or a first-grade level is meaningless, other than as a comparison from one year to another.

Standard scores, on the other hand, provide the ability to compare scores across test areas or domains to determine areas of strengths and needs. For example, in the Assessment of Adaptive Areas (Bryant, Taylor, & Rivera, 1996), which measures 10 adaptive areas, a standard score of 14 in the Community Use domain would indicate an area of student strength compared to a standard score or 6 in the Social Skills domain, and therefore yield more useful information.

After the assessments are completed, the evaluation results are reported at the IEP team meeting when the team determines and writes the Present Level of Educational Performance section of the IEP.

The following example indicates how standard scores may look from the five subscales on the Asperger Syndrome Diagnostic Scale (Myles et al., 2001):

Language	9
Social	13
Maladaptive	10
Cognitive	9
Sensorimotor	8

While all the standard scores in the above example are high enough to pronounce that there is a very strong probability of the presence of Asperger Syndrome, the standard scores allow a practitioner to reasonably suggest areas of strengths – in this case, Sensorimotor, and areas of concern, Social and Maladaptive.

Parent Issues

Consent for Evaluations

Before any school evaluation or assessment is conducted, parents must give their consent. By law, consent involves a written request to conduct specific evaluations, usually accompanied by a description of the test and an explanation of how the results will be used. If parents agree that testing should be conducted, their written consent must be returned to the school before testing can begin.

Parents should treat their consent carefully, not to be oppositional, but to make sure they fully understand the who, what, where, why, and how. Parents should also know what type of results the testing will yield and the purpose. It is perfectly within reason to ask any question you may have regarding any aspect of the testing process before signing the consent form.

Specific Concerns

It is important for parents to keep the individual characteristics of their child with ASD in mind when thinking about evaluations, especially how they are administered and how the results are interpreted and subsequently used.

Autism spectrum disorders are generally considered to be characterized by limitations in social interactions, communication, academic learning, and sensitivity to sensory input. Therefore, evaluations and assessments should address these areas using accommodations and protocol modifications where appropriate. For example, it is not unusual to provide additional time, use verbal or visual prompts, and put environmental modifications in place, such as a private work area, to assist students with ASD during evaluations.

One parent said at an IEP team meeting, "When I look at my 12-year-old son, who's able to do so many things I never thought he would be able to, it's hard to understand that his expressive communication level is so low, a 9-month level (the son was nonverbal)! He expresses himself in ways that were not tested."

The parent learned during the IEP team meeting that the expressive language assessment that had been used with her son required verbal skills. She pointed out to the team that her son communicates by gesturing, taking the hand of another person and leading him or her to an item he wants, for example. The parent asked the speech and language pathologist if her son could be reevaluated using an assessment for nonverbal children or if the pathologist could accept and administer the test in ways that would allow her son to respond with gestures and pointing. She also provided some tips for how to work with her son that were helpful to the pathologist. One particularly helpful tip was to begin each verbal prompt or direction with the child's name and wait for him to look at the pathologist before the actual prompt was presented.

> It is important for parents to keep the individual characteristics of their child with ASD in mind when thinking about evaluations . . .

When the child was reassessed taken all this into consideration, the results appeared appropriate to both the pathologist and the parent. Besides, the IEP team had more predictable information to use to develop the IEP and teaching methods.

As discussed earlier, use of grade and age equivalencies is generally discouraged unless they are subjected to careful and acute statistical analysis in an effort to understand their significance and use. For students with ASD, age and grade scores are a particular cause for concern. For example, they may demonstrate splinter skills and fluctuations between testing domains such as literacy and math, or socialization and communication. Due to the scoring procedures used for these measures, accurate scores may not be attained, making age and grade comparisons even more meaningless and non-purposeful.

Common Questions About Evaluations

Evaluations and educational assessment should not be the sole basis for constructing the IEP but can support IEP goals and objectives as well as recommendations made during the IEP meeting. Parents are encouraged to call evaluators if they have questions about an evaluation; in fact, many evaluators appreciate the opportunity to talk to the parent prior to the actual testing.

Below is a list of possible questions related to evaluations. Ask only the ones you feel are appropriate for your situation and ask only what you do not know.

- I've never heard of this test. Can you tell me something about it?

- How will you conduct this evaluation?

- Is there anything I can do to prepare my child for this evaluation?

- What information can I give you to help the testing process?

- How long will this evaluation take?

- Can you give me an example of the types of things you will be doing?

- What have you generally found when you have used this evaluation?

- What are your thoughts about this assessment? Do you like it?

- What problems have you experienced in administering this evaluation?

- How will you score the evaluation?

- How will the results be used?

- How will you report the results?

- What happens to the results?

- How will the results help me or the teachers and therapists?

- Do you feel the results have generally been accurate?

Evaluation recommendations are carefully prepared suggestions for educational program planning based on thorough analysis of evaluation data and interpretation.

Summary

Evaluation recommendations are carefully prepared suggestions for educational program planning based on thorough analysis of evaluation data and interpretation by the testing administrator. When done correctly, members of the IEP team often find the evaluation recommendations the most helpful part of the evaluation report as they provide an objective and subjective professional view of what is most important for a given student.

Many parents find it helpful to keep a running summary of evaluations conducted at school and by outside professionals such as social workers and therapists. Typically, most evaluation results are summarized under the Present Level of Educational Performance on the IEP. Recommendations from all evaluations are helpful not only for IEP development, but also for developing teaching strategies, classroom modifications, and instructional accommodations.

Too often evaluation results are only used as a basis for developing IEP goals and objectives or benchmarks. Using the Hopes and Dreams model, evaluations serve to support outcomes felt to be important by students, parents, and teachers. What parents, students, and teachers believe is most important for the family and the child's future becomes the basis for IEP development.

The worksheet on the following page will help keep professional evaluation recommendations in front of you and the IEP team as new IEPs are being developed and changes are made. By keeping this information together, you will also be able to see trends of progress in a variety of educational domains such as communication, sensory integration, vocational skills, and social skills.

HOPES AND DREAMS WORKSHEET
Summary of Evaluation Recommendations

Directions: Complete the information below whenever you have received an evaluation report. Since this will be a running summary, the date and the name or type of the instrument are important to record. Make sure to summarize recommendations into brief statements that make sense to you now as well as later when memory begins to fade and that can be interpreted by a new teacher when your child moves to a different educational environment. In the status section you can indicate accomplishments, modifications, continued interventions – anything that will help you keep track.

DATE	TEST INSTRUMENT	PROGRAM RECOMMENDATIONS	STATUS	MODIFICATIONS

Chapter 6

PARENT PREPARATION: THE HOPES AND DREAMS MODEL

In this chapter the "parent" will be referred to in the singular simply because presumably only one parent is reading this book at a time. If two parents are involved, both need to do the homework and preparation for the staffing, even if only one attends. Each household is different, so make whatever adjustments are necessary for this to make sense. For example, if the household has only one parent, one parent should do the work; if a single parent and a grandparent are involved, both need to get busy, and so on.

Approximately two to four weeks prior to any scheduled IEP meeting, such as an initial, annual, three-year reevaluation or transition meeting, you will receive a notice indicating the time, place, purpose, and invited attendees of the meeting. If it is impossible for you to attend, call the person who sent the notice and ask for another time or day, but if at all possible, make arrangements to be present according to the notice.

This notice is your warning call to get to work. Along with anyone else wearing an "I'm the expert" hat (spouse, grandparent, etc.), figure out a time when you will have one or two hours of quiet time without any other responsibilities.

FLASHPOINTS:

✔ Understanding adaptive skill areas

✔ Recognizing your child's learned and emerging skills

✔ Converting hopes and dreams into educational outcomes

✔ Being able to suggest ideas to collaborate with the school

✔ Being prepared to report at IEP team meetings

✔ Hopes and Dreams Worksheets: see pages 48, 52, 54, 59, and 63

It is OK to split this time up, so you spend one hour twice, for example. Finding time to prepare may be difficult, but it is important so, if necessary, ask for help to watch your child and/or siblings.

When you sit down to get going, review the worksheets you completed in Chapters 2 and 4. Revisit your thinking and update your worksheets as necessary. With your thinking now refreshed, you are almost ready to complete the six sequential steps of the Hopes and Dreams model, the centerpiece of this book.

But before we really get started, we need to take a closer look at the adaptive skill areas below in general terms until you (and others who are part of the process with you) are familiar with what they mean. This will provide the background for looking at your child's adaptive skills in the first step of the Hopes and Dreams model.

Adaptive Skill Areas

The adaptive skill areas listed in Table 1 are widely accepted as representing skills that most people use in their daily lives. The list was compiled from various adaptive behavior checklists, such as the Assessment of Adaptive Areas (Bryant, Taylor, & Rivera, 1996) and Adaptive Behavior Scale: School (2nd ed.) (Lambert, Nihira, & Leland, 1993).

Table 1. Common Adaptive Skill Areas

Communication
Understanding and expressing messages through either symbolic or nonsymbolic behaviors

Sensory
Sensory needs that are present or known that facilitate or interfere with learning, such as noise, light, other people, textures, smells

Academics
Skills such as basic reading, writing, and practical mathematics that are functional in today's world

Interaction
Skills necessary for appropriate socialization, including social skills, conversational exchanges, greetings

Daily Living
Activities of daily living such as eating, drinking, dressing, grooming, and toileting

Domestic
Home environment skills such as housekeeping, cooking, home safety, and appropriate use and care of money

Work
Employment (job) skills such as task completion and job learning, or chores completed around the home

Community
Appropriate use of community places such as shopping, purchasing services, and using public transportation

Self-Advocacy
Skills such as choice making, completing tasks, asking for help, problem solving, advocating one's own interests

Health
Skills such as caring for oneself, indicating illness or pain, safety skills, treatment of minor injuries

Recreation
Recreational skills involving self and others, choosing activities to participate in, appropriate recreational interactions

Assistive Technology Use
Adaptive equipment or assistive technology that facilitates learning such as computer, communication device

Step 1: Identify Learned Skills

Now that you are familiar with the adaptive skill areas, it is time to begin listing the significant skills your child has learned in each area. Review the examples on page 47 to help you complete the Hopes and Dreams worksheet on page 48. Please refer to the examples several times until a flow of ideas is coming from your heart, not necessarily your head. If you need more space to write about your child, use the back of the page or add more pages. Also, if you have access to a computer, the blank worksheets on the enclosed CD offer you lots of flexibility in terms of space.

The following example illustrates that you only have to get a single idea down, not necessarily a detailed description of an activity or task. Be proud of the adaptive skills your child has learned. Remember that no learned skill is too silly or not "professional" enough to list. This information will be essential for you to present at the IEP meeting.

Things Our Child Can Do Well *(Learned Skills)*

Communication
- ☐ Communicates wants and needs
- ☐ Uses eye gaze to indicate choice
- ☐ Labels items of interest
- ☐ Signs words, such as: _____

Sensory
- ☐ Seeks a quiet area
- ☐ Responds to various sounds
- ☐ Tolerates tooth brushing
- ☐ Responds to temperature change

Academics
- ☐ Understands danger signs
- ☐ Prints first name with model
- ☐ Tells time
- ☐ Counts to 10

Interaction
- ☐ Greets others nicely
- ☐ Rarely is aggressive toward others
- ☐ Plays with peers
- ☐ Can be redirected from self-stimulatory behavior when an unpreferred activity is presented

Daily Living
- ☐ Uses toilet with assistance
- ☐ Eats well with adaptive spoon
- ☐ Dresses appropriately for weather
- ☐ Assists with teeth brushing

Domestic
- ☐ Uses personal items appropriately
- ☐ Receives allowance and keeps money safe until he wants to buy an item
- ☐ Helps with chores

Work
- ☐ Knows how to load dishwasher
- ☐ Works with his dad in shop
- ☐ Does a daily chore
- ☐ Helps deliver newspapers

Community
- ☐ Helps when we go to the grocery store
- ☐ Stops at corners before crossing the street
- ☐ Checks for correct change
- ☐ Uses the bus
- ☐ With picture card orders at McDonald's

Self-Advocacy
- ☐ Selects choice from icons
- ☐ Asks for help when needed
- ☐ Understands morning schedule
- ☐ Completes tasks started

Health
- ☐ Signs when not feeling well
- ☐ Gets band-aid for small cuts
- ☐ Has learned not to play with electric outlets
- ☐ Knows about balanced diets

Recreation
- ☐ Can float in pool
- ☐ Plays at night with a game
- ☐ Takes turns better than last year
- ☐ Likes to sing

Assistive Technology Use
- ☐ Works well with physical structure defining his work area
- ☐ Uses separated plate at mealtimes
- ☐ Has basic computer skills
- ☐ Uses icons for choice making

HOPES AND DREAMS WORKSHEET
Information to Present During the IEP Meeting

Skills Our Child Can Do Well (Learned Skills)

Please note: You don't need to think of five skills for each area. In some cases you may have more; in others, fewer.

Communication
1.
2.
3.
4.
5.

Work
1.
2.
3.
4.
5.

Sensory
1.
2.
3.
4.
5.

Community
1.
2.
3.
4.
5.

Academics
1.
2.
3.
4.
5.

Self-Advocacy
1.
2.
3.
4.
5.

Interaction
1.
2.
3.
4.
5.

Health
1.
2.
3.
4.
5.

Daily Living
1.
2.
3.
4.
5.

Recreation
1.
2.
3.
4.
5.

Domestic
1.
2.
3.
4.
5.

Assistive Technology Use
1.
2.
3.
4.
5.

That was Step 1. Hopefully you found this insightful. It cannot be overemphasized that you should go back and look at what your child has learned before you attend any IEP team meeting. You will find it helpful to remember the things your child has learned and how those skills have been important in your child's life.

Step 2: Identifying Emerging Skills

Step 2 looks at the skills that are emerging; that is, skills that your child is starting to learn. For example, is your child starting to show some interest in the toilet or bathroom, has your child started to utter sounds, has your child started to help with routine chores, does your child watch you perform a particular task? These are all examples of emerging tasks. Emerging tasks are important because these are the skills you and the school will want to start working on to support and guide your child's development and further learning.

Think back, what has motivated you to learn different things throughout your life? Generally, you'll find that you had some interest in learning a given skill, or at least you had a concept of what it was. Remember when you put that gas barbeque grill together? It all came in a box – nothing like it was supposed to end up looking. Yet, you or someone else had an interest in putting it together (you wanted to cook out), and you had a concept of what it would be when finished (you had seen other barbecue grills).

Imagine if you had no interest in putting all those parts together and no idea of what it was supposed to be. How long would you have sat on the floor with that mammoth pamphlet of instructions and all those nuts and bolts, each one a different size? Probably not long – because you would not have been motivated to try.

Emerging skills indicate that the child either has some interest in a particular skill or has some concept of the task to be performed. Always use emerging skills as a clue of what to teach. For example, let's say your child appears to be inter-

> Emerging skills indicate that the child either has some interest in a particular skill or has some concept of the task to be performed.

ested when you are cooking the evening meal. This may be the time to engage him in some simple food preparation or asking him to set the table. Similarly, one 6-year-old girl needed help tying her shoes. When her mother noticed that the child was "messing with the laces with her hands," she quickly started teaching her daughter how to tie her shoes.

There are many things that your child cannot do, and you do not list them. They are not important at this time. Some things that your child cannot do may require you to either help or do for your child; some will necessitate that you protect and prevent your child from doing dangerous things. These skills may begin to emerge, and as parents you will have to encourage emerging skills to develop.

Usually a child needs to have some experience with or exposure to tasks and activities for an interest to develop or for emerging skills to be observable. For this reason, it is important to introduce and re-introduce activities and tasks again and again. As you expose your child to new and even familiar activities, step back and let the child explore. Long before your child can zip up his jacket, after you begin zipping it up for him, occasionally stop and see if he can perform small steps of the activity; for example, pulling it the rest of the way up after you started or knowing how to get started even if unable to actually pull.

If it appears that your child has little interest in certain activities or events, don't let that deter you. It may be worthwhile to keep re-introducing the activity or event. For example, a teenager with ASD never seemed to enjoy family picnics. During the picnic he just sat and stared, occasionally pointing to the car to signal that he wanted to go home. Finally, after several picnics he seemed to make an association between picnics and hotdogs and chips – favorite foods. Picnics have been great ever since!

Look at the following example and then complete the Hopes and Dreams worksheet *Things Our Child Is Starting to Learn* on page 52. List everything you can think of, and try to find a category to fit the emerging skill.

Things Our Child Is Starting to Learn *(Emerging Skills)*

Communication
- ☐ Starting to initiate requests
- ☐ Imitates signs
- ☐ Looks at picture cards, icons
- ☐ Responds to verbal prompts

Sensory
- ☐ Reacts to food textures
- ☐ Reacts to noise
- ☐ Indicates discomfort
- ☐ Covers ears

Academics
- ☐ Grasps pencil or crayon
- ☐ Plays with calculator
- ☐ Wants to read for enjoyment
- ☐ Points to clock

Interaction
- ☐ Has shared a toy with peer
- ☐ Waves good-bye
- ☐ Seeks less attention
- ☐ Breaks toys less frequently

Daily Living
- ☐ Grasps a spoon
- ☐ Assists in dressing
- ☐ Has been successful on toilet
- ☐ Lets me wash his face

Domestic
- ☐ Points to mess on table
- ☐ Is starting to help set table
- ☐ Helps with simple food preparation
- ☐ Points to child's schedule

Work
- ☐ Uses hammer correctly
- ☐ Wants to do a good job
- ☐ Is interested in what parents do
- ☐ Indicates work interests

Community
- ☐ Helps with shopping
- ☐ Puts token in box on bus
- ☐ Listens to stories at library
- ☐ Knows McDonald's sign

Self-Advocacy
- ☐ Looks at choices when presented
- ☐ Cries when frustrated
- ☐ Waits for a preferred item
- ☐ Stays on task longer

Health
- ☐ Looks for help at street corners
- ☐ Wants to learn CPR
- ☐ Stops before jumping in pool
- ☐ Interested in healthy foods

Recreation
- ☐ Watches children play
- ☐ Kicks at a ball
- ☐ Wants to roller skate
- ☐ Looks for something to do

HOPES AND DREAMS WORKSHEET
Information to Present During the IEP Meeting

Things Our Child Is Starting to Learn (Emerging Skills)

Please note: You don't need to think of five skills for each area. In some cases you may have more; in others, fewer.

Communication
1.
2.
3.
4.
5.

Sensory
1.
2.
3.
4.
5.

Academics
1.
2.
3.
4.
5.

Interaction
1.
2.
3.
4.
5.

Daily Living
1.
2.
3.
4.
5.

Domestic
1.
2.
3.
4.
5.

Work
1.
2.
3.
4.
5.

Community
1.
2.
3.
4.
5.

Self-Advocacy
1.
2.
3.
4.
5.

Health
1.
2.
3.
4.
5.

Recreation
1.
2.
3.
4.
5.

Assistive Technology Use
1.
2.
3.
4.
5.

Step 3: Identify Your Child's Likes and Dislikes

Step 3 involves making a list of activities, toys, games, and other things that your child likes or likes to do. While this step does not involve the development of the IEP, it lends itself to finding motivating activities and reinforcement for the child. So share the list with your child's teachers. You will find it surprising how many teachers appreciate this kind of information. Keep the list current as it will help you realize how our child's likes and dislikes change over time as a result of experiencing and being exposed to new activities. The following example is from Louis, an 11-year-old boy with Asperger Syndrome.

Things Our Child Really Likes and Likes to Do
(Interests; these can supplement teaching)

> **Keep the list current as it will help you realize how our child's likes and dislikes change over time.**

Table 2. Likes and Dislikes

- Videos
- Books about the Civil War
- Maps of Civil War battles
- Roller skating
- Shooting baskets – sometimes plays a game with his father
- McDonald's – especially French fries
- TV game shows

This list was helpful for both Louis' teachers and his parents, who started using Civil War stories as part of his reading curriculum and set up time with a history teacher to chat before school. While the interaction with the history teacher did not relate directly to Louis' IEP, it set the stage for a successful day at school.

Now turn to the worksheet on page 54. After listing as many things as you can think of, it is helpful to mark the five or so that are your child's most favorite.

This step was relatively easy and quick. The next step will take some time. It is critical that you and others wearing that "I'm an expert" hat think carefully and discuss each of the following outcomes.

HOPES AND DREAMS WORKSHEET
Information to Present During the IEP Meeting

Things Our Child Really Likes and Likes to Do
(Interests; these can supplement teaching)

1.

2.

3.

4.

5.

Step 4: Develop Outcomes

"Outcomes" are the results that you would like to have happen for your child. Remember the barbeque grill? One outcome of putting the grill together was to have friends over to enjoy your perfectly grilled hamburgers. Outcomes are measured differently than the goals and objectives that are a prominent part of the IEP. Outcomes are usually not stated in the IEP, but frame the measurable goals and objectives.

This guide is based on outcomes – the things that parents and teachers want for the child and that the child wants for him/herself. Some outcomes are defined in the school's evaluation recommendations, others are generated by the parent based on the child's hopes and dreams.

> Some outcomes are defined in the school's evaluation recommendations, others are generated by the parent based on the child's hopes and dreams.

To illustrate, let's look at the following example involving Amy, an 18-year-old young lady who wanted a job. This was her outcome. Her foster parents also wanted her to have work experience and gainful employment. This was their outcome. After some exploration, a job site was found for Amy at John's Bakery. This outcome subsequently framed the following annual (long-term) goal on Amy's IEP:

Amy will work independently at the bakery for 3 hours wrapping and pricing cookies for sale.

The short-term objectives meant to support the acquisition of long-term goals included:

1. Amy will work at the bakery with verbal prompts from the job coach to complete job assignments for one hour.

2. Amy will work at the bakery with supervision from the job coach to complete job assignments for one hour.

3. Amy will work at the bakery with supervision from the job coach to complete job assignments for two hours.

4. Amy will work at the bakery independently for 90 minutes.

5. Amy will work at the bakery independently for three hours.

Now let's take a look at how we know if goals, objectives, and outcomes are met. For goals and objectives we use frequency measurement such as "hamburgers will be grilled until done 80% of the time," or "you will grill hamburgers until you grill three in a row that are not red in the middle."

Outcomes take a different twist by involving a quality component, such as *enjoying* the company of friends when grilling burgers, or someone noticing the *good job* you did putting the grill together. Outcomes are not measured in percentages or figures. Instead, they involve something more subjective.

Think of outcomes for your child. Start with the outcomes you would like your child to reach at school, at home, in the community, and with other people. Feel free to add other types of outcomes that would be more appropriate to your child. Again, do not think of measurable goals; think about the results of the goals and objectives and how your child will use a given skill. *This is the quality factor.* These are the hopes and dreams for you and your child.

If possible, involve your child at this point. Ask your child what is important to him, what his dreams are, what he would like to do or learn to do. Some outcomes heard from children with ASD include:

"I want to learn to play the piano."

"I want a job."

"I would like to have a pet, maybe a dog; I would take care of it."

"I would like to have a credit card."

"I would like a checking account and checkbook."

"I want to ride my bike by myself."

This activity builds self-advocacy skills. (We will discuss this more in Chapter 9.) The child may say something unrealistic or improbable sounding. That's okay. At one point, I wanted to be a baseball player, and then an explorer, and no one ever told me I couldn't. I have always wondered how much I learned (and as a result, know today) because I had dreams. However unrealistic they may appear, these too are outcomes. Later exposure and experiences may help make the outcomes more obtainable and realistic. For example, I learned on my own, through experience and exposure, that I was not going to be good enough to be a professional baseball player. The explorer thing somehow went away, but was probably replaced with a love of "reading" maps.

The worksheet on page 58 asks that you think about and list the hopes and dreams you have for your child, and the outcomes your child has expressed. We may now call our hopes and dreams outcomes. The categories will help you think of important areas of your child's life: What are your outcomes for your child at home, in the community, and with other people? Have the child help you.

Before you start on your own, take a look at the following example.

> Later exposure and experiences may help make the outcomes more obtainable and realistic.

Table 3. Outcomes

The most important skills we wish our child could learn to do at home.

We wish . . .

- John would finish his evening meal at the table with the family

- John could learn to wash his hands before eating

- John would assist during dressing

- John could tell us about his day at school

The most important skills we wish our child could learn to do in the community.

- Not to yell and scream at the grocery store

- Find an activity he could do with others his own age

- Cross streets safely

- Eat at restaurants without causing others to stare at us

The most important skills we wish our child could learn to do with others (family, peers, strangers).

- Play appropriately with his brother

- Not walk up and stare at strangers

- Participate during holiday activities and meals

HOPES AND DREAMS WORKSHEET
Information to Present During the IEP Meeting

Outcomes

The most important skills we wish our child could learn to do at home.

The most important skills we wish our child could learn to do in the community.

The most important skills we wish our child could learn to do with others (family, peers, strangers).

Step 5: Review and Summarize the Worksheets: The Parent Assessment

Now to the "guts" of the whole thing. This step involves thinking about the strengths (skills already learned), the emerging skills, and the outcomes you listed previously for your child to help you formulate ideas that can be infused into the school program. This involves lots and lots of practice but following these steps will make the process easier.

To summarize the worksheets, gather the following:

1. Things Our Child Has Learned Worksheet (Step 2)

2. Things Our Child Is Starting to Learn Worksheet (Step 3)

3. List of Outcomes (Step 5)

The goal at this step is to synthesize the material from the three worksheets into a four-part summary. Section 1 is a summary of learned skills, Section 2 is a summary of emerging skills, and Section 3 is a list of outcomes relating to the home, the community, and with others. The final section is a review of the previous or existing IEP, if there is one, to summarize ideas and concerns as they pertain to the other three sections. To help you make sense of this, see the following examples of Lenny and Luke.

Luke

Luke is a 5-year-old with ASD and developmental delays. He uses nonverbal communication (eye gaze and pointing). When he is not sure of what is happening around him, he may become aggressive.

1. **Learned skills.** Luke has tolerated wearing shirts with different fabrics and he is more accepting of the noises he hears around the house (Sensory). He takes an icon for toilet when we present it to him (Communication), and he picks up his toys in the family room (Work). Luke

waves at his brother and his grandmother (Interaction), and he enjoys many more recreational activities (Recreation).

2. ***Emerging skills.*** Luke occasionally shows some awareness of the toilet icon as he goes to the bathroom (Communication, Daily Living), and he sometimes helps his brother clean plates off the table after dinner (Work). He only covers his ears when a machine sound is present, such as a vacuum cleaner or the washing machine. He no longer does so when he hears environmental sounds such as typical conversational speech or cars going down the street (Sensory).

3. ***Outcomes*** (considering interests and emerging skills) our family would like to see at home include (a) learning more home chores, perhaps cleaning his room and helping in the yard (Work); (b) learning to use the toilet by himself (Daily Living); and (c) develop some tolerance to machine sounds (Sensory). In the community we would like Luke to (a) learn to bowl (Recreation) and (b) go with his brother to the park (Interaction). With others we would like Luke (a) to play with his brother (Interaction) and (b) not to wave at everyone, even if he does not know them (Self-Advocacy).

4. ***IEP review.*** We reviewed Luke's current IEP and found that several of the speech and language long-term goals with the icons may help Luke and his brother communicate. Also, the occupational therapist and the teacher have been working on toileting and some other activities of Daily Living. Perhaps we will be able to do some of those at home also.

We did notice some new things and must be sure to tell the teacher that Luke does much better if he has time to respond to requests and if he is only given one verbal request at a time.

This step involves thinking about the strengths, the emerging skills, and the outcomes . . . to help you formulate ideas that can be infused into the school program.

Lenny

Lenny is a 13-year-old with Asperger Syndrome. He has just entered eighth grade. He prefers being alone and is preoccupied with the weather to the point that he has to know what the weather will be before he does anything, even going to bed or doing a favorite activity.

1. *Learned skills.* Lenny has done very well in middle school in most academic areas, especially math and science (Academics). Social Stories™ have been effective as part of the protocol before going into the community or engaging in interactions with same-aged friends (Interaction).

2. *Emerging skills.* Lenny is beginning to respond more appropriately to adult family members and adult friends of his parents (Interaction). While interactions with same-aged peers are difficult, Social Stories are helpful (Interaction). He is learning more about weather patterns and complicated weather forecasting (Work, Academic).

3. *Outcomes.* Lenny's preoccupation with the weather has been a drain on the family as he constantly has to know what the weather forecast is before he can do anything. Perhaps the one outcome we would like to see is Lenny learning a vocation in meteorology or a weather-related field. Maybe this will spread to some other academic areas and even some social development.

4. *IEP review.* Last year Lenny's IEP included a number of science goals; we suggest that some of the science curriculum include weather-related skills (Work). If weather were used in other academic areas, Lenny might show more of an interest in these subjects, like literacy and physical education (Academic). Another outcome would be for Lenny to develop a relationship with a scientist or a science teacher who could deal with his weather focus and maybe redirect or expand this interest to other topics and eventually help him interact more appropriately with others (Interaction).

See the Appendix, Putting It All Together, to get an idea of what the process looks like when you have completed the worksheets. Luke and Lenny are used as the examples again.

HOPES AND DREAMS WORKSHEET
Information to Present During the IEP Meeting

Ideas We Have for Coordinating Our Wishes and Dreams for Our Child with the School and for the IEP

Communication

Work

Sensory

Community

Academics

Self-Advocacy

Interaction

Health

Daily Living

Recreation

Domestic

Assistive Technology Use

Step 6: Preparation for the IEP Team Meeting

In this step, you gather all the information you have been generating for the IEP meeting. You will need the following:

1. The list of skills learned (Step 1)

2. The list of emerging skills (Step 2)

3. The list of things your child enjoys doing (Step 3)

4. The list of outcomes – hopes and dreams (Step 4)

5. The list of suggested ways to coordinate outcomes (Step 5)

Review the materials. Are you comfortable with them? You should feel good about what you have done. You have prepared very thoroughly.

Take this information to the meeting. If possible, make copies to share with the teachers and other participants. One mother who followed these recommendations emailed to tell me that the teacher and the multidisciplinary team were overjoyed with the information she presented to them. The mother was very happy, as she felt she had made a contribution, helped her son, and was a partner in the process.

In the next chapter we will look at how to best present all the information.

Chapter 7

GOING TO THE MEETING

Many parents report that the trip from home to the school for the IEP or IEP-related meeting is one of the hardest they have ever made, using words such as *anxious, nervous, scared, overwhelmed,* and *confused* to describe their feelings. Maybe you have felt the same way?

What You Have to Offer

One reason why many parents feel uneasy is that they do not know what to expect, what the teachers will say about their child, and what they will be asked to say or do. After reading this book, hopefully, you will feel differently about these meetings. You have done your homework, and you are as well prepared as the teachers and related service staff will be.

It helps to know who will be at the meeting. The list of invited participants is part of the meeting notice you received from the school. It will include the special and general education teacher, the psychologist, all related services personnel such as the speech pathologist and the occupational therapist, as well as an administrator.

FLASHPOINTS:

✔ **Presenting the parent evaluation**

✔ **The IEP team agenda**

✔ **Use of technology**

✔ **How to summarize an IEP team meeting**

✔ **Hopes and dreams**

✔ **Hopes and Dreams Worksheet:** *Notes for IEP Presentation*

You have the five lists you gathered in the last step:

1. List of learned skills

2. List of emerging skills

3. List of things your child enjoys doing

4. List of outcomes (hopes and dreams)

5. List of suggested ways to coordinate outcomes between home and school

In essence, what you have compiled is an evaluation that is not much different from the other evaluations that will be reported on during the meeting, but from your perspective. Listen as representatives from each discipline, for example, the psychologist, speech and language therapist, or the adapted physical education teacher, give their report of the assessments they have completed. Each will summarize strengths revealed by the assessment (*learned skills*), identify needs as seen by the evaluator (*emerging skills*), describe any observations made during the assessment process (*interests*), present conclusions drawn from the evaluation (*outcomes*), and make recommendations for service delivery (*coordination of outcomes*). Your evaluation brings a new dimension to the IEP format, as it is a composite of all evaluations and a real-life test of what skills your child has learned and used.

In the truest sense of the word generalization, your evaluation measures if your child is actually using the skills learned at school, home, with others, at day camp, at the city recreation program, or anywhere else. This is extremely important; in fact, it is the most important aspect of education. For example, if your child has been learning at school to not repeat questions over and over to strangers, this skill may have met some level of mastery in the classroom. *But the real test is whether your child uses the skill during naturally occurring activities* – at the grocery store, on the bus or with relatives. To answer this question, your evaluation (emerging skills) is important and presents a new dimension at the IEP meeting.

Well, back to the meeting with your completed homework

(evaluation) – and that knot in your stomach. Some time before the meeting begins, tell your child's teacher or the person chairing the meeting that you have some information you would like to present. Do this by arriving a few minutes early and mentioning it to the teacher or person running the meeting or by making a telephone call the day before or on the day of the meeting. Don't do this three weeks in advance, as it is likely to be forgotten in the meantime.

Going First or Last on the Agenda?

As the meeting begins, decide when you want to take your turn. Do you want to go first, or do you want to wait till the end? This is your decision. By going early you can set the tone for the entire meeting. Your presentation of your homework with copies available for the school staff will make a huge impression. The school staff will experience some of the same anxiety you may have. Hearing your presentation, the school staff will be impressed, and you should sense collaboration growing in the room.

Generally, present first if you feel that your information will set the tone for the team meeting. If your information is significantly different from what you expect to hear from others, or if you desire to focus the emphasis of the team meeting on something new, you may find success in presenting first.

When I chair IEP team meetings, I like it when the parent and the student express their thoughts early in the agenda as it creates a movement or a theme from which to work. What the student has to say is very important, and the IEP team should hear this first.

The other option, of going later on the meeting agenda, will have a different effect. As your evaluation is a composite of all the other evaluations and one that really addresses generalization, it makes for a nice summary! Presenting after the other IEP team members has an advantage that you are able to synthesize school evaluations and recommendations and fold this information or data into your presentation. That is, you are

Your presentation of your homework with copies available for the school staff will make a huge impression.

able to use evaluation data to support parent and student outcomes, making your presentation a meaningful summary.

Either way, you, the school, and your child are much further ahead thanks to your advance preparation.

One parent wanted to hear everyone's report before she spoke at her son's IEP team meeting. After hearing all the data and recommendations, she reported that everything that was said seemed accurate, but the team had missed what was most important! She said she heard the occupational therapist report about her son's improved fine-motor skills and the teacher reporting about his successful community experiences, but what was most important to her was for her son to be able to drink appropriately from a glass. She went on to say that when she takes her son out to eat with the family, he slurps from his glass and spills most of the liquid down the front of his shirt. This causes nearby diners to stare at him and the family – "it affects the quality of our time together," she commented. She summarized that the fine- and oral motor skills were present and that her son had practiced them but that generalization was missing and that this was something the school and she could work on together. They did.

How to Do It

To decide "What do I say?" when starting your report, all you have to do is say, "My husband/wife and I (or whatever fits your situation) have been doing some thinking about this IEP and we put some thoughts together (following a plan we found in a book" – if you think the reference to a publication will make it easier for you). "We wrote some things down in five categories, and we would like to share them with you."

This is the time to pass out copies of your materials and review concisely each of the five lists you have completed. You do not have to go into great detail, just quickly summarize the skills learned, the emerging skills, the interests, your child's and your outcomes (the hopes and dreams!), and some ideas for how the school and you can work together. With a little practice, you should be able to do this in less than 10 minutes. You will not be minimizing the importance by being brief! The school personnel will carefully read your written worksheets and will appreciate that you do not go into detail on every item.

The key is to highlight and practice ahead of time what you want to say. Most evaluation reports minimize their effects after about 10 minutes, as listeners are not able to concentrate for much longer than that. Make sure you do not ramble on. To get a sense of what is appropriate, the best advice is to listen to others give their reports. The best ones are concise, include personal observations, and give some clear evidence for any recommendations made. If you or anyone else wants more, you / they can go back and read the report later.

The key is to highlight and practice ahead of time what you want to say.

If you have given your evaluation summary early in the meeting, listen to the recommendations of the reports that follow yours. Are you able to make any connections to your outcomes? Can you envision any collaborative efforts between home and school? Do the reports sound like the information you shared? Can you pick up where some skills have not generalized? Jot some of your observations down on a notepad.

If you are giving your report last or later in the agenda, listen carefully throughout and answer some of the same questions. When your turn comes, you will be in a perfect spot to confirm or question previous recommendations. *Remember, the goal is to gain a collaborative IEP, one that is not only effective at school but that carry over to home, the community, and with other people.*

If you disagree with anything said in the meeting, do so, but do not go overboard. This happens too often, especially when parents do not have any evidence to stand on. After doing your homework, you have reliable evidence and can simply ask to discuss the recommendations, or results, or findings because you arrived at a differing viewpoint when you completed your worksheets. Say, for example, "We feel differently about Kimberly's use of eye gaze. When we looked at this area, we found ..." This is evidence, and is substantiated documentation! You can now discuss the issue based on both sets of documentation – yours and that of the school staff – without anger and frustration resulting in an emotional response. Such an approach makes for an intelligent discussion of differences. Your child benefits.

Typical Agenda Items

Every school has its own meeting agenda format, every district has its own forms, and every state has its own vocabulary and rules. Regardless of the terminology and format, the following must be addressed in the IEP meeting.

1. *Statement of the student's Present Level of Functioning as found in observations and measurable terms such as grade or age levels.* Example from Luke found in the Appendix (page 109): Using parts of the Brigance test, Luke demonstrated general knowledge skills between 1.0 to 2.5 year level. Strengths were demonstrated in matching, and weaknesses in body part recognition.

2. *Evaluation results and findings that eventually support long-term goals and short-term objectives.* These results are often included in the Present Level of Functioning.

3. *Proposed or projected long-term goals with some reasonable assurance that the goal can be met in about a year.* Short-term objectives may be proposed, but they can never be finalized before the IEP meeting. Example from Luke: Luke will increase academic skills by three months as measured on the Brigance (see page 109).

4. *Assessment of assistive technology, if applicable.* These may include some of the things you wrote down on your worksheets, such as communication devices, sensory items, and so on. Schools are required to conduct an assessment for assistive technology. Such assessments

review a comprehensive array of low and high technology and attempt to match known technology to the needs of the student. High technology may include things like augmentative communication systems, voice output devices, specialized adaptations for motor utilization, and computerized assistance. Low technology may include adaptive drinking cups, plates with separated compartments, visual schedules in classrooms and work stations or even in other parts of the school and at home, and headphones. The lists for both are endless.

5. *Discussion of related services.* This may include occupational therapy, recreation, speech, social work, and the degree to which your child is included in general education. If a related service is necessary, it must be written into the IEP. This section usually includes duration and frequency of the related service provided. In Luke's example, the occupational therapist may recommend OT three times a week for a total of 45 minutes, speech and language twice a week for 60 minutes, and counseling on a consult basis.

6. *A description of transition planning toward adulthood.* This applies if your child is between the ages of 14-16 years and older, depending on the state rules (see Chapter 9).

7. *Extended school year, or ESY.* This area must also be addressed, as must identification for Braille instruction and orientation and mobility. ESY is typically provided when a regression of skills has been demonstrated over periods of time. Check with the local school district to find out about the specifics of summer school or ESY. Braille and mobility/orientation instruction relates to students who are visually limited.

Schools are required to conduct an assessment for assistive technology.

Sample Agenda

All schools have their own agendas. While they are similar, I generally follow this agenda during IEP team meetings.

1. Welcome, state the purpose of the meeting (for example, an annual IEP review, three-year reevaluation, placement or change of placement, transition, quarterly). I then outline what the goals are for the meeting, such as to develop a transition plan, to review the goals and objectives for an annual IEP review.

2. Introduce all members present and the respective roles each will play during the meeting.

3. Ask the student and/or the parents if they would like to present any information or make any opening comments.

4. Hear reports or evaluation summaries from all related service personnel and classroom teachers, including program recommendations.

5. Discuss future or new long-term goals based upon the outcomes from parents and school staff and discuss corresponding short-term objectives.

6. Discuss ESY, assistive technology, and ascertain related service minutes per week, duration, frequency, and location of services.

7. Summarize the actions of the IEP team meeting.

8. Specify when the team will meet again and thank everyone for participating.

   As the agenda nears its end, I highly recommend that you ask to summarize the meeting with the following questions, or something similar as appropriate for your situation:

   - How can we, as parents, and you, as teachers, work together in teaching the objectives on the IEP?

   - What things will the teachers do and what will we

do for each of the objectives? (This question may also be directed to each of the related services professionals recommending services after their report.)

- How will all of us (parents and teachers) know about progress and communicate problems?

- When will the next evaluation or meeting take place, and what would you like us (parents) to provide?

These questions are confirming; not confrontational. They underscore your intention to work together – with teachers and the entire school – and indicate that you are interested in evaluating the success of the IEP both at school and at home. This is exactly what teachers would want to see happen.

Finally, end the IEP meeting with a statement similar to the following:

"Thank you! Thank you for helping (your child's name) learn how to achieve his or her hopes and dreams. We greatly appreciate this opportunity to work together in developing this IEP (placement decision, evaluation) for our son/daughter. We are looking forward to seeing what we can do as a team to enhance the quality of life and the future for our child and your student. Let's keep in touch."

This is the goal! You successfully integrated home and school, collaborating at every step with the school personnel. And it was done within the letter and the spirit of the law. I believe this was what the founders of P.L. 94-142 had in mind back in 1974 – even though it took until 1997 for parents to be included as "equal partners" in the IEP process.

The following worksheet is for you to jot notes for each category to assist you in preparing and presenting your information to the IEP team. These notes will also serve as a great summary and point of reference when you begin the next IEP cycle.

You successfully integrated home and school, collaborating at every step with the school personnel.

HOPES AND DREAMS WORKSHEET
Notes for IEP Presentation

My child has recently learned:

I have seen my child use these skills (in the following situations):

My child uses these skills (*frequently, sometimes, only when* or *in certain situations*):

My child is beginning to (emerging skills):

I have seen this when:

These emerging skills are occurring *frequently, sometimes, only when* or *in certain situations*:

My child really enjoys:

I have prepared a list of outcomes that are very important to me and my child. These were developed using my child's acquired and emerging skills and things that my child really likes to do:

I have prepared several ideas for how we can coordinate outcomes between home and school:

Chapter 8

THE "RULES" – COLLABORATION IS THE KEY

This chapter is not about the rules of the Individuals with Disabilities Education Act or your local district rules or regulations for special education. It is about rules for interactions between parents and school personnel to build a successful and collaborative IEP.

The IEP process is not about parents getting as many services for the greatest length of time for their child, nor is it about meekly watching the IEP being developed in front of you only because you think the school people know best. The process outlined in this book is about sharing ideas and working together to make the IEP effective for your child and their student; nothing more and nothing less.

To make the IEP process work collaboratively, parents and teachers must understand each other. In Chapter 2 and 3 concerns from parents and teachers were identified as a first step in breaking down barriers and understanding the perspectives of both parties. If you will recall, there were many points of agreement and similarity.

There are only three key rules for collaboration in the IEP

FLASHPOINTS:

✔ **The attributes of collaboration**

✔ **How to collaborate effectively with the school**

✔ **Collaboration means building a meaningful relationship**

✔ **Hopes and Dreams Worksheet:** *My Suggestions for Collaborating and Building Great Home-School Relationships*

process that you need to remember. Following these rules will bring about the greatest success imagined. Our goal is specific outcomes for the student or child – the hopes and dreams – and this is accomplished by collaboration, cooperation, and participation.

Let us look at the three rules and how best to follow them.

Rule #1: Respect Time and Commitments

Every time a group of parents who have children with ASD gather, one of the first things that come up is how busy they are and how there's never time enough in the day. There probably has never been a parent of a child with ASD who is not busy and barely has time to do the most basic of things, including a little relaxation from time to time.

The same is true for teachers. If you review the teacher comments found in Chapter 3, you will see that time is the number one concern. Teachers feel they do not have time enough to develop social skills curriculum, create visual schedules, or set up sensory areas in a resource room. Yet, every special education teacher not only has to do these things, he or she also has to generate lesson plans, monitor IEP objectives, conduct evaluations, and attend countless meetings. Parents and teachers are in the same boat and both have expressed that time is a very frustrating factor.

Parents must respect the time teachers have available to do their job, just as school personnel must be respectful of parents' time. Teachers have other students who need their attention, and often parents have more than one child who needs their attention. As a result, most teachers never "just put in the hours," and most parents cannot say, "that's enough for the day, I'm done."

How Best to Follow Rule #1

- If you need to talk to the teacher or some other school staff member, call and make an appointment even if you have to wait a day – the results will be better.

- Expect to be flexible about when IEP meetings or conferences are scheduled.

- If you can send a note to school or email a concern, you may receive a quicker response than by playing phone tag and leaving a line of messages between the school secretary and your answering machine. If you do not have your own computer, you can go to a nearby library. Most libraries have computers that allow you to send emails; if you have not entered the techno world, someone will be happy to help you.

- Expect a response within a reasonable length of time.

- If you have a face-to-face meeting, make sure your thoughts are organized – and use your worksheets! It is a huge waste of time for you and the teacher to try to figure out what the question is or what the concerns are without a basis for discussion. Also try to have a reasonable solution to your concerns.

- Expect teachers and school staff to give you undivided attention during the face-to-face meeting and make a sincere effort to work out any concerns within the power of the person with whom you are meeting.

- If you are talking on the phone or meeting with a staff member, or even if you are writing a note or email, keep your message to the point and make it as short as possible. Also, deal with only one or two issues at a time.

- Expect clear, concise, and informative responses or interactions from the teacher or the school staff member.

If you need to talk to the teacher or some other school staff member, call and make an appointment

Rule #2: Everyone Is an Equal Partner

The reauthorization of IDEA clearly states that parents are equal partners in the IEP process. That is, your voice is as important as anybody else's! But we need to be precise here. If a teacher were to say "yes" with documentation and a parent said "no" with evidence (your completed worksheets), that is equal. However, sometimes the teacher (or other school personnel) says "no" and the parents retorts, "Yes, but I am the parent and you can't tell me that. I demand this. My child deserves it, and that's it!" This is not equal partnering. Nor is it being equal if the parent says, "Whatever you say, I'm not the expert, so I guess what you say makes the most sense."

Equal partnering means equal say, upon the condition that each partner has done equal homework. This is why the preparation for the IEP you did in Chapter 6 was so important. Having completed those five worksheets makes you the equal partner the IDEA encourages all parents to be. In other words, completing the worksheets lets you put on the "I'm an expert" hat.

Equal partnering seeks uncompromising solutions. Equal partners respect other opinions, and equal partners share information toward a common goal – you know this by now – the hopes and dreams! Aristotle believed goodness is found between two evils. Similarly, equality is found between aggressiveness and passiveness. Equal partnering is a delicate balancing act.

How Best to Follow Rule #2

- If you have an opinion, back it up with evidence from the information you gathered for the worksheets.

- Expect other opinions to be backed by documentation or logic.

- If you disagree, disagree with respect to the evidence or documentation presented, not by using personal attacks or meaningless emotional responses.

- Expect others to disagree, presenting documentation or evidence in support of their argument, not by passing judgment on you or your parenting.

- If you do not understand why a given recommendation or statement was made, ask for an explanation.

- Expect a respectful and well-thought-out response.

- Remember, if you are not wearing your "I'm an expert" hat, no one will put it on for you.

- Expect the school personnel to know what they are talking about or doing.

- Say what you believe and expect others to also say what they believe. This is what both you and the teachers want. This is collaboration, and this is what leads to a successful IEP.

Rule #3: Share to Build Relationships

The main concept in all of these pages has been to share. Parents share what they observe at home, in the community, away from the structure at school, and with other people. Teachers (or other professionals) share what they observe through the structure of a learning environment, with peers, and through assessments and evaluations. These are different vantage points, and information will therefore vary. One setting cannot function without the other, so it only makes sense to share what happens at each.

Sharing also takes another spin that is frequently overlooked. Parents and teachers come from very different angles in one important sense. Parents love their child. Therefore, they sup-

One setting cannot function without the other, so it only makes sense to share what happens at each.

port, defend, and advocate out of love for their child. Teachers do not love the child in the same way. Teachers care about the child as a student among other students. Both want the best, both reach for student potential, both wish success – but parents' love brings different reactions and methods than teachers' encouragement of a child in a group of students. Parents should love their child and teachers should care about all the students in their class. It is essential to recognize that the teacher will never love your child the way you do, and you will never care about all the students your child is placed with the way a teacher does.

As you walk into the school or talk with a teacher, only your loved one is on your mind. When the teacher is talking to you, the teacher sees your child objectively as one individual among other students he or she cares about equally. Be aware that sometimes your love for your child will cloud your objectivity. Sharing is going to be a delicate balance between two points of view, and these points of view must be understood by both partners to benefit the child or student.

Sharing is building a relationship, a triangle of your child, the teacher, and you. During the course of your child's schooling, several (or many) relationships may have to be built, but it is essential that the relationship between all points of the triangle be developed. This is where sharing comes in. As parents share information (such as the worksheets) and teachers share information, the relationship develops. Many times the parents have more information about their child's ASD, interventions, and strategies than the teacher. This is not a reason to berate the teacher, but a time to share. Develop good working relationships with the school personnel who have contact with your child, and be open to relationship building initiatives from the teacher. Your purpose together for the child is to share – not win.

How Best to Follow Rule #3

You know what to do, but let's briefly review:

- Share your worksheets with your child's teacher ahead of any IEP team meeting.

- Share the joys, frustrations, and challenges you feel comfortable sharing with your child's teacher(s).

- Share information that you have learned doing your own research as well as at conferences and meetings that you have attended.

- Expect to attend several meetings with school personnel before seeing signs of a collaborative relationship.

- Share information in a non-threatening manner; never in an angry or condescending way.

- Ask the teacher(s) to share insights and thoughts.

The following worksheet is a chance for you to write down ways that YOU think will build relationships and encourage home-school collaboration. There are two lists: one for specifying what you can do and another for what you expect from the school. As your relationship flourishes, share your lists with teachers and school staff. Their comments and ideas can add tremendous power to developing meaningful relationships, collaboration, and your child's success.

Sharing is building a relationship, a triangle of your child, the teacher, and you.

HOPES AND DREAMS WORKSHEET
My Suggestions for Collaborating and Building Great Home-School Relationships

WHAT I CAN DO	WHAT I EXPECT FROM THE SCHOOL

Chapter 9

THE SCHOOL YEARS AND BEYOND: SELF-ADVOCACY AND TRANSITION PLANNING

Our hopes and dreams guide our lives. Think back to how your own hopes and dreams began to form in your mind. For many of us, they matured and developed from other hopes and dreams. Remember my dream to be an explorer? This dream probably came from some childhood idea or experience I can no longer recall, but the explorer dream remains very clear. This dream evolved into doing something new and exciting; finding a new frontier. My frontier throughout my professional career has been to write something new. I am now pursuing my dream.

The same is true for hopes and dreams for our children. Their dreams cannot be our dreams, and we cannot live their dreams, but as parents we must expose our children, with and without disabilities, to experiences that can potentially build dreams, and let them evolve and develop. Exposure to new things builds dreams through an expression of interests.

FLASHPOINTS:

✔ Introduction to self-advocacy

✔ How to use transition planning to prepare for your child's future

✔ When to start discussing transition planning

✔ Who to involve in transition planning

✔ Hopes and Dreams Worksheet: *Transition Contacts*

This chapter will provide an overview of self-advocacy, explain the interaction of the transition plan and the IEP team, and offer ideas for parents to consider and carry out in preparation for and implementation of transition planning.

Self-Advocacy

Self-advocacy relates to the ability to determine how we would like to live our life, make life choices that are meaningful, and express likes and dislikes. Self-advocacy is an important activity for everybody. Yet, in the past self-advocacy was typically not made available or encouraged for persons with many disabilities, primarily because it was not felt that they were able to perform such activities.

Only in the past 20 years have efforts been made to allow persons with disabilities to advocate on their own behalf. Since that time, instruction has gradually been introduced to help persons with disabilities to self-advocate. Instruction in self-advocacy includes understanding of human rights, decision making, citizenship, and life choices such as marriage, having children, driving a car, and owning a home.

Parents and teachers should work together to help children/students become self-advocates. Many guides are available for home and school instruction and experiences (see examples under Resources). The following discussion only serves as an introduction.

Watch your child engage in a favorite activity. How is she communicating to you that this is something fun or pleasurable? Encourage this expression and allow the child to create or imagine anything she wants to. Such communication is an expression of self-advocacy. *Self-advocacy needs to develop and mature much like dreams do.* Self-advocacy supports the pursuit of our dreams.

As we have repeatedly stressed in this book, the IEP is about the hopes and dreams of your child. Therefore, it should include your child's interests and the things he has communicated as being important. As the child becomes a young adult, the hopes and dreams should be the backbone of his education. That probably is your hope and dream too.

Transition Planning

Transition services are often misunderstood by parents, and many times also by school district representatives. It is important that parents become knowledgeable about what transition services are, who determines transition services, and how and where they are provided.

Briefly, transition services are meant to facilitate the move from K-12 education into post-school opportunities through a coordinated set of activities. This involves much more that the team using existing long-term IEP goals to develop a transition plan. Transition is a process of student, parents, teachers, and potential adult service and agency representatives coming together to discuss what will happen in the future, how to get there, and what skills or attributes are necessary for the student to successfully move into adult life.

Many parents report that transition services are either an afterthought following an IEP team meeting or that the transition plan is simply constructed from existing IEP goals and objectives. In other words, the transition planning function is completely backwards from what it should be.

Transition planning should be the emphasis of IEP team meetings after the student has reached age 14. This means that the team meeting begins with a discussion of what plans or ideas parents, the student, and the school staff have for the student after K-12. If a direction is determined, such as technical school or college, work, or the military, the remainder of the team meeting should be focused on developing an IEP and goals and objectives that will support the skills the student will need to successfully reach these goals. After the goals and objectives are discussed at an IEP team meeting, they are aligned in a transition report to support a postsecondary goal.

Self-advocacy relates to the ability to determine how we would like to live our life, make life choices that are meaningful, and express likes and dislikes.

When parents and school personnel are working together and when IEP team meetings are collaborative, the transition planning will be smooth and coordinated and produce successful strategies for students entering adult life.

When starting transition planning it is important to get input from postsecondary and adult service agencies. As with the IEP itself, parents are encouraged to think what possibilities may be available for their child, and the student should dream what her future would look like.

Transition planning should start as early as possible. The law (IDEA, 1997) requires the IEP team to begin discussing transition at age 14 and transition planning to begin when the student is 16, but it allows planning to start earlier when necessary. With the current human service and postsecondary education issues of budget constraints, waiting lists, and program cuts, earlier is almost always necessary.

It is recommended that by the time the student is 14 discussions are going on and that an initial transition planning meeting is scheduled at the IEP team meeting closest to age 14. This meeting is set up by the school district, similar to the way in which previous IEP team meetings were scheduled. The members of the IEP team initially continue on the team, but as the transition plan becomes clearer, others are invited and encouraged to attend and become part of the team. These "new" team members include representatives of adult and postsecondary agencies and organizations such as counselors from Vocational Rehabilitation, admission officers from two- and four-year colleges, and agency representatives from adult living services.

This transition planning meeting may be held in conjunction with an IEP team meeting, but the transition discussion and planning must be the first focus of the meeting. The initial meeting is to discuss options and your hopes and dreams. Is postsecondary education on the horizon, or is vocational training more appropriate? Are you thinking of social support groups or adult living arrangements?

During this first transition planning meeting, the team should be discussing the potential of your hopes and dreams, and those of your child, and who should be involved in future transition planning meetings. Remember, the transition planning process is a coordinated set of activities that must include instruction, community experiences, and the determination of vocation or employment or other postsecondary adult living outcomes.

How can an IEP team plan instruction and experiences when the needs to enter adult services are unknown? This is a critical concern of transition, and postsecondary representatives must be available to answer questions such as the following:

1. What skills and experience does the student need in all the domain areas?

2. What skills and experience are necessary to be successful in any adult services or postsecondary education?

3. What skills and experience does the student need to acquire before leaving K-12?

The answers to these questions will lead the IEP team to purposeful transition planning.

Don't think that starting at age 14 or 15 is too soon. Starting early gives postsecondary adult services time to get involved. The participation rate of representatives from postsecondary, vocational, and adult living agencies is not stellar. For example, it is not uncommon to hear that the student must be an adult before a relationship with adult services can be established, and far too often when the student graduates or becomes an adult, her name is just added to a waiting list. The same may be experienced with postsecondary education admission counselors. This is why starting early is important. While it may not be possible to determine a final path for adult services at age 14 or 15, the direction should be discussed. It may even be possible for adult service representatives to offer ideas of what adult requirements will be.

> The transition planning process is a coordinated set of activities that must include instruction, community experiences, and the determination of vocation or employment or other postsecondary adult living outcomes.

Often parents and teachers can do some preparation work during this time. For example, information such as admission requirements and eligibility criteria may be obtained and shared with the IEP team. In this connection, it is important to understand that by moving from K-12 education to adult services, the student is going from an entitlement program (public education) to an eligibility-based service. That is, services are no longer automatic and require self-initiation.

Of course, the important question is: What does the student want to do? This is where self-advocacy, also referred to as self-determination, comes in. Hopefully, through the experiences of his K-12 education, your child has developed a sound ability to self-advocate so that when you ask, "What do you want to do when you are an adult," the answer is not only a hope and a dream, but a meaningful expression of a thought-out plan, or at least the beginning of one.

The purpose of the transition meeting is to identify skills and experiences necessary for successful movement from secondary education into adult living services, vocational experiences, and postsecondary education. The team will assess the student's skills and experiences in these areas and plan for the relevant instruction and experiences to be included in the IEP team document. Transition planning goes outside of the one-year box commonly in place for IEP team meetings; multi-year planning is necessary. Likewise, the IEP team must think outside of the K-12 education system box and focus on more than educational outcomes.

In preparation for transition planning, it is recommended that students and parents:

1. Find out who at the local district is in charge of transition planning.

2. Ask to look at the form or paperwork designed by the district for transition planning.

3. Begin exploring what the student would like to do as an adult.

4. Check out human service, vocational, and postsecondary opportunities.

After the first transition planning meeting:

1. Develop a contact list of agency representatives and communicate with them regularly.

2. Make sure the IEP objectives are leading in the right direction.

3. Continue to ask your child about her hopes and dreams. Remember, her ideas will wander like any teenager's dreams, but keep her in the process and encourage the continual development of her future goals.

4. Express your hopes and dreams and align your child's experiences and outcomes with your and your child's dreams.

Many schools maintain directories of available and appropriate sources, and some schools have begun to hold transition exhibitions to involve and connect parents and representatives from postsecondary services and options. Parents may also wish to start their own search relative to their child's needs and identified outcomes.

The following are suggestions for who should be contacted and asked to be involved in transition planning:

- Admission counselors from two- and four-year colleges and universities

- Local office of the Department of Vocational Rehabilitation

- County offices of State Departments of Human or Social Services

- County mental health services

- Workforce Development and local business development groups

> By moving from K-12 education to adult services, the student is going from an entitlement program (public education) to an eligibility-based service.

- Adult living services, local or county offices

- Social Security Administration

- Recreational and leisure time organizations and services

- Transportation organizations

Develop a resource notebook of contacts made with all appropriate services. Use the worksheet on following page as a guide.

HOPES AND DREAMS WORKSHEET
Transition Contacts

Date	Person Contacted	Agency	Services Provided	How to Follow Up	Follow Up

HOPES AND DREAMS

Hopes and Dreams is simply about that – the hopes and dreams we all pursue for meaningful lives. Unfortunately, persons with disabilities often face obstacles when trying to pursue valuable and personalized goals. To a certain extent we may need to accept recent issues of educational funding and testing mandates that may create barriers to individual accomplishment, but what we do not have to accept is the misrepresentation of autism spectrum disorders common in our society, which is responsible for many walls blocking hopes and dreams.

We must tear down the walls of ignorance, denial, and disrespect by continuing to make many small contributions to our world about the dignity of all people and the abilities and talents everyone has to offer. Our frustration, discouragement, and hopelessness cannot be the standard to display to society. Our standard must be the exuberance and joy of our children pursuing their hopes and dreams.

Thank you for sticking with me through this guide. My hope and dream is for you to find success using it. This field is growing quickly, and research is looking at many aspects of autism spectrum disorders, so we cannot rest on where we

We must tear down the walls of ignorance, denial, and disrespect by continuing to make many small contributions to our world about the dignity of all people and the abilities and talents everyone has to offer.

are today. You, I, the teachers, occupational and speech therapists, the vocational trainer, and the guy down the street can all come together as we help your child seek his or her hopes and dreams.

If this guide has helped one parent, or one child, or one teacher, actualize a hope or a dream, the hopes and dreams of the author and this effort have been immeasurably realized.

REFERENCES

Brigance, A. H. (1999). *Brigance diagnostic comprehensive inventory of basic skills.* North Billerica, MA: Curriculum Associates.

Brownwell, R. (2000). *Receptive one-word picture vocabulary test.* Novato, CA: Academic Therapy Publications.

Bruininks, R., Woodcock, R., Weatherman, R., & Hill, B. (1996). *Scales of independent behavior, revised. Comprehensive manual.* Chicago: Riverside Publishing.

Bryant, B. R., Taylor, R. L., & Rivera, D. P. (1996). *Assessment of adaptive areas.* Austin, TX: Pro-Ed.

Dunn, W. (1999). *Sensory profile.* San Antonio, TX: Harcourt Brace Jovanovich.

Harrison, P. (1985). *Vineland adaptive behavior scales: Classroom edition manual.* Circle Pines, MN: American Guidance Service.

Hoover, H. D., Hieronymus, A. N., Frisbie, D. A., & Dunbar, S. B. (1996). *Iowa tests of basic skills.* Chicago: Riverside Publishing.

Gilliam, J. E. (1999). *Gilliam autism rating scale.* Austin, TX: Pro-Ed.

Kaufman, A., & Kaufman, N. (1985). *Kaufman test of educational achievement.* Circle Pines, MN: American Guidance.

Krug, D. A., Arick, J. R., & Almond, P. J. (1993). *Autism screening instrument for educational planning* (2nd ed.). Austin, TX: Pro-Ed.

Lambert, N., Nihira, K., & Leland, H. (1993). *Adaptive behavior scale-school* (2nd ed.). Austin, TX: Pro-Ed.

Myles, B. S., Bock, S. J., & Simpson, R. L. (2001). *Asperger Syndrome diagnostic scale.* Austin, TX: Pro-Ed.

Psychological Corporation. (2003). *Wechsler intelligence scale for children-IV.* San Antonio, TX: Harcourt Brace Jovanovich.

Roid, G., & Miller, N. (1997). *Leiter international performance scale-Revised.* Chicago: Stoelting.

RESOURCES

Bateman, B. D., & Linden, M. A. (1998). *Better IEPs: How to develop legally correct and educationally useful programs* (3rd ed.). Longmont, CO: Sopris West.

Grandin, T., & Duffy, K. (1994). *Developing talents: Careers for individuals with Asperger Syndrome and high-functioning autism.* Shawnee Mission, KS: Autism Asperger Publishing Company.

Pierangelo, R., & Jacoby, R. (1996). *Parents' complete special education guide: Tips, techniques, and materials for helping your child succeed in school and life.* West Nyack, NY: Center for Applied Research in Education.

Shore, S. (Ed.). (1994). *Ask and tell: Self-advocacy and disclosure for people on the autism spectrum.* Shawnee Mission, KS: Autism Asperger Publishing Company.

Twachtman-Cullen, D., & Twachtman, R. J. (2002). *How well does your IEP measure up?* Higganum, CT: Starfish Specialty.

Waltz, M. (1999). *Pervasive development disorders: Finding a diagnosis and getting help.* Cambridge, MA: O'Reilly.

APPENDIX

PUTTING IT ALL TOGETHER

The following pages are examples of what the results of the completed process may look like. The two examples are based on the brief descriptions of Luke and Lenny on pages 60-62.

Luke is a 5-year-old with autism and developmental delays. He uses nonverbal communication (eye gaze and pointing), and when he is not sure of what is going on, he may become aggressive.

Learned Skills	Emerging Skills	Outcomes
COMMUNICATION – uses several icons for familiar and preferred items; uses eye gaze and points to get desired items	Utters more sounds; will take icon for toilet; uses sounds to get attention	1. Use icons outside of home 2. Make sounds into words
SENSORY – covers ears when sounds are uncomfortable; tolerates environmental noise	Covers ears when near vacuum or washing machine; looks for help when uncomfortable	1. Tolerate machine noise 2. Less sensitivity to different clothing fabrics
ACADEMICS – matches shapes and colors; stacks rings in proper order; holds pencil and crayon and traces lines	Helps sing alphabet song and mimics counting; starting to trace curves on paper	1. Learn alphabet 2. Learn numbers 3. Print his name
INTERACTION – waves "hello" and "good-bye" to others; enjoys being with his brother, but does not play with him	Follows brother in play areas; occasionally smiles at familiar persons; watches people socialize	1. Play with brother 2. Go to a "Y" program 3. Increase appropriate social skills with others
DAILY LIVING – can now use a fork to stab food; drinks from a glass; lets an adult brush teeth; dresses self except for closures and zippers	Assists with tooth brushing, bathing, and grooming; pulls at zipper; is occasionally successful on toilet	1. Use toilet 2. Brush teeth with minimal assistance
DOMESTIC – does not show much interest in home-making or money	Nothing seen at this time	None

Learned Skills	Emerging Skills	Outcomes
WORK – picks up toys when asked; is aware of several chores and knows when they are done	Occasionally helps brother clear table after meals	1. Help more with chores 2. Complete "job" at school
COMMUNITY – associates eating with some fast food places; knows he gets a treat at grocery store	Observes in community; enjoys riding in car and going places	1. Learn to do a community activity
SELF-ADVOCACY – seeks help when needed; knows what he wants and often points toward the desired item	Seems to understand that two icons provide a choice, but he grasps both if they are preferred	1. Learn to make choices 2. Greet only people he knows
HEALTH – points to ears, head, or stomach when he hurts	May lie down if not feeling well	1. Understand need for safety in community
RECREATION – enjoys activities with his grandmother	Watches brother play	1. Participate in the "Y" kids bumper bowl program
ASSISTIVE TECHNOLOGY – uses icons and a suction plate	Looks at the computer	1. Use a computer

School and Home Coordination: We would like the school to address academic and computer outcomes that we can implement at home. We can work together in developing choice making, socializing with others, appropriate social skills, toileting, and the use of icons. Speech should work on vocalization and increased use of icons, and let us know how to support these efforts at home and in the community. We would also like some strategies for community safety and increasing chores at home. Help is needed from occupational therapy to desensitize sensory issues and set up ways to learn daily living skills at home and school.

Ideas We Have for Coordinating Our Wishes and Dreams for Luke with the School and for the IEP

Communication – We need to coordinate the icons used at home and at school; we would like to see cookie, walk, and stop added. We need to do what the speech therapist is doing with vocalizations and sound productions at home.

Sensory Issues – Please be aware of white and environmental sounds around classroom areas. Need to be concerned with textures, especially clothing and the art smock neck strap.

Academics – We have been singing the alphabet song and counting on fingers, how do you do these things? What are we going to do to start printing? We've tried the fat pencil, but finger coordination seems to be a problem. Can the OT help?

Interaction – Let's develop a positive behavioral approach for aggression toward others that can be used in the community as well as at home and school. Can the school encourage playing with peers during playtime?

Daily Living – We need to be more consistent with toileting. We have to teach him to initiate picking up the icon and being successful; has to be the same at school and at home. What ideas do you have for zipping and buttoning? What can you do about the motor skills?

Domestic – none.

Work – Can Luke be assigned a daily task to do at school?

Community – Luke enjoys the school outings. A variety of community recreation would be great.

Self-Advocacy – We need a consistent approach to help him not greet everyone. We have tried to provide two choices hoping he would select one, but he picks both. We should both try to teach choice making.

Health – Should be teaching safety on the school outings.

Recreation – In P. E. learn bowling or ball rolling.

Assistive Technology – Start to teach a computer program. Provide access to a touch screen. We will also try at home. Do you recommend any programs that will reinforce alphabet or numbers?

Lenny is a 13-year-old with Asperger Syndrome. He has just entered eighth grade. He prefers being alone and is preoccupied with the weather to the point that he needs to know what the weather will be before he does anything, even going to bed or doing a favorite activity.

Learned Skills	Emerging Skills	Outcomes
COMMUNICATION – has good communication skills but hei s shy and does not verbalize much. He writes notes and letters	Beginning to grasp some abstract concepts	1. Encourage consistent verbalizations 2. Instruct in abstract concepts
SENSORY – no known needs	No known needs	
ACADEMICS – great interest in math and science; gets good grades in everything except social studies and physical education. Reads weather and some science books at home	Higher-level math and natural sciences, especially weather-related topics are of interest. Reading on these topics has recently increased	1. Use weather to reinforce other learning
INTERACTION – Social Stories™ have been successful in preparing Lenny for social situations and community events, as well as more appropriate interactions with family	Interest in the sciences; wants to be with someone who can talk about weather and science topics	1. Arrange regular time with a teacher or a scientist to learn and practice social skills and interactions
DAILY LIVING – all skills are present	—	—
DOMESTIC – spends and saves money; little interest in home making	—	—
WORK – completes some tasks asked of him; refuses to complete at times if he does not want to do task	Little interest in vocations but seems more aware of different kinds of work	1. Develop ideas for weather-related jobs

Learned Skills	Emerging Skills	Outcomes
COMMUNITY – uses community services and is independent	–	–
SELF-ADVOCACY – indicates appropriate choices; expresses wants and needs	Participates in IEP meetings	1. Teach more appropriate behaviors to refuse doing things he does not want to do
HEALTH – skills are present	Wants to take CPR	
RECREATION – plays on computer by himself; reads science and weather magazines	No known emerging skills	1. Increase variety of leisure-time activities with others

School and Home Coordination: The academic and behavior outcomes can be coordinated at home and at school. Is there a science teacher at school who could spend some time with Lenny once or twice a week on a regular basis to discuss weather, science, and math and how these areas may be career paths for him? Parents will seek recreation opportunities with peers, if school could reinforce with Lenny being in groups where he can be successful. Will other content-area teachers be willing to use science and weather concepts in their classes?

Ideas We Have for Coordinating Our Wishes and Dreams for Lenny with the School and for the IEP

Communication – Teach abstract concepts.

Sensory Issues – none.

Academics – Use weather and math as appropriate to help teach social studies, literacy, and phys. ed. We would like to support Lenny's interest in reading magazines on weather and science.

Interaction – Can you locate a teacher or a scientist whom Lenny can begin to develop a relationship with and socialize with during or after school? We feel this will help Lenny learn new social skills and also be fun for him. Social Stories™ should be used more during the school day.

Daily Living – none.

Domestic – none.

Work – Weather and science may be viable vocational interests; we should encourage him to explore as much as he can with these topics; field trips and special projects would be helpful.

Community – none.

Self-Advocacy – We have to develop a consistent approach to his refusal to do expected tasks. He should be given more opportunities to speak during the IEP meetings, perhaps even learn to chair the meeting.

Health – Does the school provide CPR training?

Recreation – In P. E. learn more social and life-long activities.

Assistive Technology – Would the school and a teacher be interested in developing a weather station or a science club that Lenny could participate in?

SAMPLE IEP

JONESVILLE SCHOOL DISTRICT
INDIVIDUAL EDUCATION PROGRAM

Name: Luke   Date of Birth: 2/1/98   Page: 1 of 8

IEP Beginning Date: 9/12/03   IEP Ending Date: 9/11/04   M-Team Due: 9/12/05

Area of EEN/Diagnosis: Autism, Speech/Language Delay

Educational Coordinator: Larry Jones

School of Attendance: Oak Street Elementary

A. Statement of the specific educational services and the amount of time for each service, frequency, location, and duration (if different from the ending date).
      Special education – 200 minutes per week in the classroom and community
      Specially designed physical education – 90 mpw in gym and community

B. Are there any related services required?   X   YES   _____ NO

Service	Amount	Frequency	Location	Duration
Occupational Therapy	45 mpw	3 x week	Classroom	Year
Speech/Language	60 mpw	2 x week	Classroom	Year
Physical Therapy				
Health Services				
Social Work				
Audiology				
Counseling/Psychological	consult	as needed		
Educational Interpreting				
Orientation/Mobility				
Transportation	50 mpw	2 x week		Year

C. If visually handicapped, does student need:
Braille Instruction: NO
Orientation and Mobility: NO

D. Does the child have communication needs?   X   YES   _____ NO
If yes, describe: Luke uses multiple modalities to communicate wants and needs, including a combination of gestures, vocalizations, and visual displays. Most vocalizations relate to attention seeking.

E. Is the student deaf or hard of hearing? _____ YES __X__ NO
    Is an interpreter needed? _____ YES __X__ NO

F. Does the student need assistive technology services or devices? ___ YES _X_ NO

G. Are transition services required? _____ YES __X__ NO
    If yes, see attached Summary of Transition Services

H. Does the student require a formal behavior program? __X__ YES _____ NO
    If yes, please attach to IEP.

I. Does the student require extended school year to prevent regression of skills?
    __X__ YES _____ NO

    Luke requires extended school year as he has demonstrated regression of skills
    during the summer months.

K. Will this student participate in regular education? __X__ YES _____ NO
    If no, explain amount of time outside of regular education participation:

L. Will this student participate in standardized testing? _____ YES __X__ NO
    The IEP team agreed that alternative testing is most appropriate

Supplemental Aids and Supports (supports provided to Luke to ensure success with this
IEP and his personal outcomes):

   1. Beware of sudden machine noise in learning environments.
   2. Encourage peer interactions in all environments.
   3. Assign several small chores for Luke to do during the day.
   4. Use the adapted smock (with no neck straps) during art classes.
   5. Encourage social greetings (wave, walking up to people) only with people
       known to Luke.
   6. Provide opportunities for choice throughout the day.

Name of Student: Luke   **Service Integration:** Classroom, music, S/L (Home)

Present level of educational performance: Luke currently uses multiple modalities to communicate wants and needs, including a combination of gestures, vocalizations, visual displays (icons). Recent testing placed receptive skills at about 2 years of age, and expressive language at 6-8 months.

Measurable annual goal: Luke will increase receptive and expressive language skills to appropriately make and respond to requests in 10 situations daily.

Procedures for measuring progress toward the annual goal: Daily data collection and charting, observation, annual performance assessment. Parents will be notified of progress during the quarterly review and written summary.

Objectives (N=New, M=Met, R=Revised, C=Continued)

Quarter	Annual	2nd	3rd	4th
Date	9/12/03			
1. Luke will identify 10 functional icons given a choice of 3 and respond when asked, "show me __," with 70% accuracy.	C – 43%			
2. Luke will follow simple one-step directives during activities given verbal and gestural cues with 75% accuracy.	C – 30%			
3. Luke will use multiple modalities (vocals, gestures, visual displays) to spontaneously communicate the following language functions with 70% accuracy: a. Greetings b. Requesting objects c. Affirmation/rejection	N			
4. Luke will appropriately choose a preferred activity 90% of the time when choices using icons are offered to him.	N			

Name of Student: Luke   **Service Integration:** Classroom, OT (Home)

Present level of educational performance: Using parts of the Brigance test, Luke demonstrated general knowledge skills between to 1.0 to 2.5 year level. Strengths were demonstrated in matching, and weaknesses in body part recognition.

Measurable annual goal: Luke will increase academic skills by 3 months as measured on the Brigance.

Procedures for measuring progress toward the annual goal: Daily data collection, observation, performance assessment, and monthly reviews. Parents will be notified of progress during the quarterly review and written summary.

Objectives (N=New, M=Met, R=Revised, C=Continued)

Quarter	Annual	2nd	3rd	4th
Date	9/12/03			
1. Luke will point to named body parts (mouth, eyes, nose) with 80% accuracy.	C – 51%			
2. Luke will match 6 objects by color with 90% accuracy.	C – 83%			
3. Luke will point to 6 named colors with 90% accuracy.	N			

4. Luke will demonstrate understanding of the following quantitative concepts with the Laureate First Categories program each with 90% accuracy:
  a. many vs. few
  b. little vs. big
  c. empty vs. full
	
	C – 72%
	C – 62%
	N			

5. Luke will identify his printed name from a group of 3 with 90% accuracy	N			
6. Luke will form a horizontal line on paper, moving from left to right covering the paper for 8 of 10 trials.	N			
7. Luke will hold writing utensil in an adaptive grasp for 8 of 10 trials.	N			

Name of Student: Luke   **Service Integration:** Classrooms, all areas (Home)

Present level of educational performance: Inappropriate behaviors interfere daily in all environments. Physical aggression averages 43.5 times per week with 0.6 episodes documented as severe. Self-injury averages 3.2 times per week with 0 documented as severe. Agitated disruptive behaviors average 42.7 times per week. Luke prefers to play alone and really enjoys music.

Measurable annual goal: Luke will increase appropriate social behaviors in all environments by 25% over baseline.

Procedures for measuring progress toward the annual goal: Daily charting of social behaviors, monthly review, quarterly reporting with written summary. Quarterly reporting to parents.

Objectives (N=New, M=Met, R=Revised, C=Continued)

Quarter	Annual	2nd	3rd	4th
Date	9/12/03			
1. Luke will decrease episodes of physical aggression to an average of 32.75 or less per week for 4 consecutive weeks.	C – 43.5 times per week			
2. Luke will decrease episodes of self-injury to an average of 2.5 or less per week for 4 consecutive weeks.	C– 3.2 x per week			
3. Luke will decrease episodes of agitated disruptive behaviors to an average of 32 or less per week for 4 consecutive weeks.	C – 42.7 x per week			
4. Luke will participate for at least 10 minutes in a variety of leisure activities during planned free time on his schedule for 8 of 10 sessions.	N			
5. Luke will interact with peers during recess following visual review of play expectations once daily for 5 minutes or more for 8 of 10 recess periods.	N			

Name of Student: Luke   **Service Integration:** Classrooms, OT (Home)

Present level of educational performance: Using the Adapted Behavior Scale (ABS), Luke demonstrated skills in the range of <3.0-9.0 years with strengths in physical development and prevocational activity and weaknesses in independent functioning, economic activity, language development, numbers and time, self-direction, and socialization.

Measurable annual goal: Luke will increase functional life skills by 3 months as indicated on the ABS (self-care, play/leisure, and community domains).

Procedures for measuring progress toward the annual goal: Daily charting of performance, monthly review, quarterly reporting with written summary. Quarterly reporting to parents.

Objectives (N=New, M=Met, R=Revised, C=Continued)

Quarter	Annual	2nd	3rd	4th
Date	9/12/03			

1. Luke will put on the following articles of clothing requiring closures with 90% success over a 4-week period:
   a. Pants or shorts
   b. Shirt
   c. Jacket
   d. Velcro-closed shoes
	N			

2. Luke will take off the following articles of clothing requiring closures with 90% success over a 4-week period:
   a. Pants or shorts
   b. Shirt
   c. Jacket
   d. Velcro-closed shoes
	N			

3. Luke will be taken to the bathroom on a 90-minute schedule and will void 70% of the time for 4 weeks.	C – 36%			

4. Luke will assist with the following hygiene tasks with 50% participation for 4 weeks:
   a. Face washing
   b. Teeth brushing
	N			

LUKE'S BEHAVIOR PLAN

TARGET BEHAVIORS

Physical Aggression: includes scratching, kicking, hitting, and biting. Luke will sit on the floor and kick his feet when he is upset, if sudden machine noises occur, or when others are too close by. If others are within his personal space, they may be kicked, but he does not go out of his way to kick aggressively. Aggression may be toward a person he is displeased with, who has placed a non-preferred demand on him, or who is in close proximity.

Potentially Severe Aggression: includes aggression that is likely to or has caused injury; non-redirectable. Aggression tends to be non-severe in nature.

Self-Injurious Behaviors (SIB): include biting his wrist, hand banging, hitting self on head. Self-injury occurs most likely when sensory needs are not met (e.g., noise, clothing textures) or if he feels uncomfortable with others.

Potentially Severe Self-Injury: includes SIB that is likely to or has caused injury: non-redirectable. SIB tends to be non-severe in nature.

Agitated/Disruptive Behaviors: include vocal vocalizations, crying, running around immediate environment, climbing on furniture. Typically, agitated and disruptive behaviors occur in demand situations or when a less than preferred activity is presented to him. Transitions are difficult for Luke, and agitated behaviors usually occur if adequate preparation time is not provided before transitions.

ANXIETY-LEVEL BEHAVIORS
Loud vocalizations

ANTECEDENTS
Not getting his way
Not feeling well/sick
Transitions, especially when he is not given lead time
Unsure of expectations
When he has to urinate but doesn't want to "let it go"
Hungry or thirsty
Noises; especially a vacuum and power tools
Tired

LIKES

Listening to music
Swinging
Getting lightly scratched
Sandbox
Dry oatmeal to touch and run hands through
Baths

BEHAVIOR APPROACHES

1. Offer lead time prior to terminating or changing activities. He is accustomed to be given "5 minutes" and then subsequent reminders (ex: 3 minutes, 1 minute) before changing activities.

2. If Luke engages in target behaviors, staff will attempt to decrease outside stimulation to provide him the opportunity to calm himself. For example, encourage him to go to a quieter area, turn off TV or radio, and limit the number of people present. Parents have given him the prompt that "It's OK" when he is beginning to calm. Be careful not to inadvertently reinforce the acting-out behavior by offering too much condolence.

3. Once behaviors have escalated, they may need to "run the course." Encourage Luke to self-remove to a quiet area away from others.

4. Redirect him to a task or activity prior to behaviors becoming out of control.

5. Redirect him back to task or activity after episodes of target behaviors.

OTHER

Sensory – swinging, light scratching, singing, climbing, balance beam. Mother reports she sings to him and lightly scratches his arms when he goes to bed. Luke will rock back and forth on hands and knees to self-calm.

SAMPLE IEP

JONESVILLE SCHOOL DISTRICT
INDIVIDUAL EDUCATION PROGRAM

Name: Lenny_____   Date of Birth: 2/1/90_____   Page: 1 of 3_____

IEP Beginning Date: 9/2/03___ IEP Ending Date: 9/1/04_____ M-Team Due: 9/12/04

Area of EEN/Diagnosis: Autism / Asperger_____

Educational Coordinator: Lucy Jones_____

School of Attendance: Jonesville Middle School_____

A. Statement of the specific educational services and the amount of time for each
   service, frequency, location, and duration (if different from the ending date).
       Special education – 60 minutes per week in the classroom and community
       Science teacher interaction – 30 minutes per week in science lab

B. Are there any related services required?   __X__ YES   _____ NO

Service	Amount	Frequency	Location	Duration
Occupational Therapy	consult	15 min. monthly	Classroom	Year
Speech/Language	30 mpw	1 x per week	Classroom	Year
Physical Therapy				
Health Services				
Social Work				
Audiology				
Counseling/Psychological	consult	15 min. monthly		Year
Educational Interpreting				
Orientation/Mobility				
Transportation				

C. If visually handicapped, does student need:
   Braille Instruction: NO
   Orientation and Mobility: NO

D. Does the child have communication needs?   __X__YES   _____ NO
   If yes, describe: Lenny is able to use verbal language to communicate effectively. He
   does not fully grasp abstract concepts and pragmatics.

E. Is the student deaf or hard of hearing?   _____ YES   __X__ NO
   Is an interpreter needed?   _____YES   __X__ NO

F. Does the student need assistive technology services or devices? _____ YES __X__ NO

G. Are transition services required? _____ YES __X__ NO
   If yes, see attached Summary of Transition Services

H. Does the student require a formal behavior program? _____YES __X__ NO
   If yes, please attach to IEP.

I. Does the student require extended school year to prevent regression of skills?
   _____ YES __X__ NO
   Lenny does not require extended school year as he has not demonstrated regression of skills during the summer months. Parents have followed any recommendation from the team meetings to provide a consistent summer approach to behavioral and educational strategies.

K. Will this student participate in regular education? __X__ YES _____ NO
   If no, explain amount of time outside of regular education participation:

L. Will this student participate in standardized testing? __X__ YES _____ NO
   The IEP team agreed that Lenny can participate in grade-level state testing.

Supplemental Aids and Supports (supports provided to Lenny to ensure success with this IEP and his personal outcomes):

1. TEACCH structure and visual schedules during all waking hours.
2. Use of Social Stories™ to teach social skills.
3. Mr. Jenkins, the science teacher, will invite Lenny to come to his classroom before classes and print out a daily weather forecast for the school and include current barometric pressure, wind direction, temperature, and sky conditions.
4. OT will monitor sensory issues and provide a sensory-appropriate diet for Lenny during lunch and his study period.

Name of Student: Lenny   **Service Integration:** Classrooms, Speech, (Home)

Present level of educational performance: Lenny demonstrates age- and grade-level communication and uses verbal communication effectively in all areas except social conversations. Use of Social Stories™ has helped Lenny stay on topic and maintain conversational interactions.

Measurable annual goal: Lenny will increase conversational skills with adults and peers by spontaneously maintaining communication exchanges five times in natural settings.

Procedures for measuring progress toward the annual goal: Daily charting of performance, monthly review, quarterly reporting with written summary. Quarterly reporting to parents.

Objectives (N=New, M=Met, R=Revised, C=Continued)

Quarter	Annual	2nd	3rd	4th
Date	9/12/03			
1. Lenny will not talk to strangers while in the community with 1 verbal reminder 90% of the time	C – 80%			
2. Lenny will appropriately carry on a conversation for at least 3 communication exchanges, remaining on topic, and making eye contact 80% of the time.	C – 65%			
3. Lenny will demonstrate an understanding of abstract concepts using pictures and hypothetical situations 70% of time.	N			
4. Lenny will appropriately carry on a conversation for at least 5 communication exchanges, remaining on topic, and making eye contact 80% of the time.	N			
5. Lenny will appropriately interpret facial expressions modeled by a teacher 80% of the time (pragmatic skills).	N			

WORKSHEETS

HOPES AND DREAMS WORKSHEET
Getting Organized

✔	File Topics	Filed (date)
	Notices of IEP team meetings	
	School evaluation reports	
	Determination manifestation (eligibility)	
	File for initial IEP with progress summaries	
	File(s) for each successive IEP with progress summaries (Keep three years' worth of IEP updates and other supporting IEP materials until a three-year reevaluation is completed. Then start a new three-year cycle.)	
	Copies of Hopes and Dreams worksheets each time completed	
	Copies of any related medical evaluations and reports	
	Copies of any related professional evaluations and reports	
	Behavioral notes	
	Progress notes of significant and not-so-significant events you feel are special and noteworthy	
	Selected photographs or other materials you feel demonstrate success	

K. Lentz, Hopes and Dreams: An IEP Guide for Parents of Children with ASD ©2004.
Shawnee Mission, KS: Autism Asperger Publishing Company. www.asperger.net. Copied with permission.

HOPES AND DREAMS WORKSHEET
How Do You Feel about Parenting Your Child with ASD?

Directions: Write your thoughts for each question.

1. What has been the most difficult or frustrating issue you have faced as a parent of a child with autism spectrum disorders?

2. What has been your most successful accomplishment or experience as a parent of a child with an autism spectrum disorder?

3. What is missing?

4. What ideas do you have to do things differently?

5. What do you do for yourself to relieve stress or to relax?

K. Lentz, Hopes and Dreams: An IEP Guide for Parents of Children with ASD ©2004.
Shawnee Mission, KS: Autism Asperger Publishing Company. www.asperger.net. Copied with permission.

HOPES AND DREAMS WORKSHEET
Parent-Teacher Communication

Directions: Write down your thoughts. You will not need to share this with anyone. Refer to it frequently and revise it as necessary. Review it prior to any meeting with your child's teacher(s).

What are my hopes and dreams for my child?

Am I comfortable sharing my hopes and dreams with my child's teacher? If not, why?

My "short list" of concerns (I need to start a little slow at this point).

My "short list" of what I wish would happen (I do not have to go overboard here as I want to build a better relationship with the teacher).

Some issues are not the school's responsibility. Which ones?

If the teacher and I could work on something together, what would it be?

K. Lentz, Hopes and Dreams: An IEP Guide for Parents of Children with ASD ©2004.
Shawnee Mission, KS: Autism Asperger Publishing Company. www.asperger.net. Copied with permission.

HOPES AND DREAMS WORKSHEET
Memories of Past IEP Meetings

Directions: Think about previous IEP meetings you have attended and answer the questions below. If you have never attended an IEP meeting, review the questions anyway and try to imagine how you may feel.

What did I like about some of the IEP meetings?

How did I feel before and during the meetings?

What made me feel uncomfortable?

When was my input requested?

What contributions did I make at the meeting?

Did I feel good about the outcome?

Did I feel the needs of my child were met?

How could the meeting have been different?

How could I have been more helpful as the parent expert?

HOPES AND DREAMS WORKSHEET
Summary of Evaluation Recommendations

Directions: Complete the information below whenever you have received an evaluation report. Since this will be a running summary, the date and the name or type of the instrument are important to record. Make sure to summarize recommendations into brief statements that make sense to you now as well as later when memory begins to fade and that can be interpreted by a new teacher when your child moves to a different educational environment. In the status section you can indicate accomplishments, modifications, continued interventions – anything that will help you keep track.

DATE	TEST INSTRUMENT	PROGRAM RECOMMENDATIONS	STATUS	MODIFICATIONS

K. Lentz, Hopes and Dreams: An IEP Guide for Parents of Children with ASD ©2004.
Shawnee Mission, KS: Autism Asperger Publishing Company. www.asperger.net. Copied with permission.

HOPES AND DREAMS WORKSHEET
Information to Present During the IEP Meeting

Skills Our Child Can Do Well (Learned Skills)

Please note: You don't need to think of five skills for each area. In some cases you may have more; in others, fewer.

Communication
1.
2.
3.
4.
5.

Sensory
1.
2.
3.
4.
5.

Academics
1.
2.
3.
4.
5.

Interaction
1.
2.
3.
4.
5.

Daily Living
1.
2.
3.
4.
5.

Domestic
1.
2.
3.
4.
5.

Work
1.
2.
3.
4.
5.

Community
1.
2.
3.
4.
5.

Self-Advocacy
1.
2.
3.
4.
5.

Health
1.
2.
3.
4.
5.

Recreation
1.
2.
3.
4.
5.

Assistive Technology Use
1.
2.
3.
4.
5.

K. Lentz, Hopes and Dreams: An IEP Guide for Parents of Children with ASD ©2004.
Shawnee Mission, KS: Autism Asperger Publishing Company. www.asperger.net. Copied with permission.

HOPES AND DREAMS WORKSHEET
Information to Present During the IEP Meeting

Things Our Child Is Starting to Learn (Emerging Skills)

Please note: You don't need to think of five skills for each area. In some cases you may have more; in others, fewer.

Communication
1.
2.
3.
4.
5.

Sensory
1.
2.
3.
4.
5.

Academics
1.
2.
3.
4.
5.

Interaction
1.
2.
3.
4.
5.

Daily Living
1.
2.
3.
4.
5.

Domestic
1.
2.
3.
4.
5.

Work
1.
2.
3.
4.
5.

Community
1.
2.
3.
4.
5.

Self-Advocacy
1.
2.
3.
4.
5.

Health
1.
2.
3.
4.
5.

Recreation
1.
2.
3.
4.
5.

Assistive Technology Use
1.
2.
3.
4.
5.

K. Lentz, Hopes and Dreams: An IEP Guide for Parents of Children with ASD ©2004. Shawnee Mission, KS: Autism Asperger Publishing Company. www.asperger.net. Copied with permission.

HOPES AND DREAMS WORKSHEET
Information to Present During the IEP Meeting

Things Our Child Really Likes and Likes to Do
(Interests; these can supplement teaching)

1.

2.

3.

4.

5.

HOPES AND DREAMS WORKSHEET
Information to Present During the IEP Meeting

Outcomes

The most important skills we wish our child could learn to do at home.

The most important skills we wish our child could learn to do in the community.

The most important skills we wish our child could learn to do with others (family, peers, strangers).

HOPES AND DREAMS WORKSHEET
Information to Present During the IEP Meeting

Ideas We Have for Coordinating Our Wishes and Dreams for Our Child with the School and for the IEP

Communication

Work

Sensory

Community

Academics

Self-Advocacy

Interaction

Health

Daily Living

Recreation

Domestic

Assistive Technology Use

K. Lentz, Hopes and Dreams: An IEP Guide for Parents of Children with ASD ©2004.
Shawnee Mission, KS: Autism Asperger Publishing Company. www.asperger.net. Copied with permission.

HOPES AND DREAMS WORKSHEET
Notes for IEP Presentation

My child has recently learned:

I have seen my child use these skills (in the following situations):

My child uses these skills (*frequently*, *sometimes*, *only when* or *in certain situations*):

My child is beginning to (emerging skills):

I have seen this when:

These emerging skills are occurring frequently, sometimes, only when or in certain situations:

My child really enjoys:

I have prepared a list of outcomes that are very important to me and my child. These were developed using my child's acquired and emerging skills and things that my child really likes to do:

I have prepared several ideas for how we can coordinate outcomes between home and school:

HOPES AND DREAMS WORKSHEET
My Suggestions for Collaborating and Building Great Home-School Relationships

WHAT I CAN DO	WHAT I EXPECT FROM THE SCHOOL

HOPES AND DREAMS WORKSHEET
Transition Contacts

Date	Person Contacted	Agency	Services Provided	How to Follow Up	Follow Up